JUNE

June–August 2019
Vol. 61, Issue No. 4

My Devotions

Daily Readings for Young Christians

Contributors to the June devotions:

Nicole Dreyer, Jim Gimbel,
Diane Grebing, Cheryl Honoree, Steve Teske

Edited by Mark S. Sengele

JUNE

1

• • • • • • • • •
Saturday
• • • • • • • • •

Oh sing to the LORD a new song, for He has done marvelous things! His right hand and His holy arm have worked salvation for Him. The LORD has made known His salvation; He has revealed His righteousness in the sight of the nations.

Psalm 98:1-2

A New Song

What was the last new thing you did? Did you play a new game? read a new book? try a new kind of food? What was the last new thing you got? Was it a shirt? a pair of shoes? a game or a book?

Most people enjoy new things. God must like new things too. In Psalm 98, we read, "Sing to the LORD a new song" (v. 1). Does that mean we have to make up a new song to sing to God every day? If we had to write songs all the time, our songs would probably start to sound the same.

Jesus once told His followers that He was giving them a new commandment. He told them to love one another. God had been telling people to love one another for a long, long time.

The word *new* means something different when God says new. When God talks about a new song or a new commandment, He means that He is making us new. We sometimes make things old when we do not do what is right. When we say things we shouldn't say or do things we shouldn't do, our lives are worn out and do not seem new.

In Baptism, Jesus makes us new again. There, we receive the gifts of His salvation. Even though we sin every day, God forgives us every day. This makes everything about us new, even our songs that we sing to the Lord.

Journal:

What will you do today because you are new? It can be something you've done before!

Pray:

O God, on this first day of a new month, I thank You, because I know You have made me a new person. Thank You for making me new each day. Help me to sing a new song to You today and tomorrow and every day. Amen.   *S. T.*

Turtle Troubles

"Mom," Herbie called as he ran into the house, "is it okay to pray for a turtle?"

"What do you mean, 'pray for a turtle'?" his mother asked.

"When Grandpa and I were working outside with our shovels, we hit a turtle. At first, we thought it was a rock. I think we hurt it. Does God mind if I pray for that turtle?"

Herbie's mother smiled. "God does not mind if you pray for a turtle. In fact, He wants us to care about the world He made, even turtles."

Herbie frowned. "But is God too busy to care about little turtles?" he asked. "Will He be unhappy if I bother Him about something so small?"

"God invites us to pray about anything. Nothing is too big for Him, and nothing is too small for Him. I think the only thing about our prayers that makes God sad," Mom continued, "is that sometimes we forget to pray to Him."

"Does God really want us to talk to Him anytime? Sometimes when I want to talk to you, you tell me that you are too busy."

Ask, and it will be given to you; seek, and you will find; knock, and it will be opened to you. For everyone who asks receives, and the one who seeks finds, and to the one who knocks it will be opened.

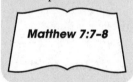

Matthew 7:7–8

"I know I say that sometimes, but God is almighty. That means He can do anything, anytime. He can hear and answer all our prayers. The Bible even tells us to 'pray without ceasing'" (1 Thessalonians 5:17).

"Then I'm going to go say another prayer to God about the turtle. I hope it gets better." Herbie ran back outside.

Through faith in Jesus, Herbie, his mom, you, and I can call God our Father and come to God in prayer. Turtles, temptations, tests—the topics don't matter.

Journal:

What small thing have you recently prayed about?

Pray:

Jesus, thank You for inviting me to pray in Your name and come to my heavenly Father with any request. Help me to remember to pray often. Amen.   S. T.

Test the Spirits

Beloved, do not believe every spirit, but test the spirits to see whether they are from God, for many false prophets have gone out into the world. By this you know the Spirit of God: every spirit that confesses that Jesus Christ has come in the flesh is from God.

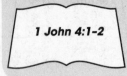

1 John 4:1-2

Some children go to Lutheran schools. Other children go to public schools or private schools, and some children are taught at home by their parents. Wherever you go to school, you probably have tests—all kinds of tests. There are spelling tests, math tests, physical fitness tests, reading tests, science tests, social studies tests, music tests, and more. You study or practice to take all these tests.

You probably know how to do other tests too. You can test batteries and lightbulbs to see if they work. You may take just a taste of milk to test it. No one likes to drink sour milk! Maybe you've even taken a test drive on a new bike.

When John told his readers to test the spirits, he wasn't thinking of a school exam, batteries, or milk. He means we should compare what someone is telling us about Jesus or the way to heaven with the clear teachings of the Bible. This is truly an important test.

As John says, many false prophets have gone out into the world. There have always been tricky people who lie. Even the devil disguises himself. So it is no surprise that he leads others to give false messages.

So when you hear a new idea about Jesus or about how to get to heaven, check it out. Look to God's Word. It is inspired and inerrant, meaning without any errors. Look to Jesus. He is the only Savior of all people. He and He alone paid for the sins of the world on the cross. That's the truth.

Journal:

What is the way to test a message about God?

Pray:

Dear Jesus, keep me from believing false teachings about You. Thank You for the truth of Your Word and for the people who help me learn about You. Thank You for being my Savior. Amen.   *S. T.*

God Knows Your Name

Are you good at remembering names? Name the person who sat by you at lunch on the first day of school last year. What was your great-grandmother's first name? Do you know the first name of your dentist? What was the name of your first stuffed animal?

The Bible mentions many people by name. It tells us a lot about some people but very little about others—maybe only their names.

The Book of 1 Chronicles begins with names. It lists people by their families and generations, but it tells us almost nothing else about them. No one expects you to remember the names of Simeon's sons.

Although we may not remember their names, those brothers are still important to God. In fact, every person is important to God. Jesus died for the sins of Nemuel and his brothers. Jesus wanted to forgive their sins and include them in His kingdom. Even after all these years, Jesus has not forgotten them. Those who trusted Jesus' promises are with Him now and awaiting the Last Day, when He will make everything new.

The sons of Simeon: Nemuel, Jamin, Jarib, Zerah, Shaul; Shallum was his son, Mibsam his son, Mishma his son. The sons of Mishma: Hammuel his son, Zaccur his son, Shimei his son.

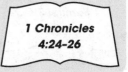

1 Chronicles 4:24–26

Why do we care about Nemuel and his brothers? When we remember that Jesus knows them and loves them, it comforts us. Jesus knows us and loves us too. After all, He is our Savior. He died on the cross for us. Through faith, He gives us the gifts of salvation. He forgives our sins and includes us in His kingdom.

Journal:

Which name in the Bible do you find strangest or funniest? How does God feel about the person who had that name?

Pray:

Thank You, Jesus, for making me Your child in Baptism. Thank You for being my Savior and for the gifts You give to me. Amen.   *S. T.*

JUNE

5

Wednesday

Then the LORD called Samuel, and he said, "Here I am!" and ran to Eli and said, "Here I am, for you called me." But he said, "I did not call; lie down again." So he went and lay down.

1 Samuel 3:4–5

Samuel!

Can you imagine sleeping in a church? Can you imagine your bed being within a few yards of the altar? What would you do if one night you heard the voice of God calling your name?

That happened long ago to a boy named Samuel. He was living with Eli, the priest at the tabernacle. At night, he slept not far from the ark of the covenant, which was a holy object. The room where the ark was kept was so special that no one was supposed to be there. Only the high priest was allowed in there, and he was allowed to go in there only once a year.

One night as Samuel slept, God called him by name. He gave Samuel work to do. He gave Samuel messages to share with God's people, including a promise of punishment.

We are sinful people and deserve God's punishment for breaking His rules. But Jesus paid for our sins on the cross. In Holy Baptism, God called us by name and promised to forgive our sins. Now that we are forgiven, God gives us work to do. Part of that work is to share the good news of His forgiveness with other people who have broken His rules.

How good it is that God called Samuel by name. How good it is for us that God loves us and calls each of us by name.

Journal:

Write something important that Samuel did. If you don't remember anything about Samuel, ask someone else about him.

Pray:

Jesus, thank You for loving me. Thank You for forgiving all my sins. Thank You for calling me by my name. Amen.   S. T.

Nobody Knows

Maria dropped her schoolbooks on the table and ran into the kitchen, where Dad was cooking supper. "Dad, Consuela says that the world is going to end soon. She says we shouldn't bother doing homework, because the world is about to end."

Dad stirred the beans and checked the rice. "Where did Consuela get this interesting information?" he asked.

"She says it's in the Bible, Dad. Does the Bible really say that the world is going to end soon?"

"Well, let's see what the Bible really says," Dad answered. Then he continued, "Jesus did say He was coming soon, but He didn't say what 'soon' means. It's already been hundreds of years since Jesus said that." Dad found the verse he wanted Maria to see. "Look right here. Jesus says nobody knows the day or the hour. It might be today or tomorrow. It might not be for many, many years."

But concerning that day or that hour, no one knows, not even the angels in heaven, nor the Son, but only the Father. . . . And what I say to you I say to all: Stay awake.

Mark 13:32, 37

Maria read the verse and other verses near it. "A lot of frightening things are going to happen," she said.

"Yes, they are frightening, but they've been happening for hundreds of years, Maria. We've had wars and all the rest going on for a long time. But guess what? Jesus is still in control. On the cross, He paid for the sin that causes these things. When He comes again, the world will be perfect, just like He promised."

Maria sighed. "Does that mean that Consuela and I still have to do our homework?"

Dad nodded. "That's right, kiddo. You still have to do your homework."

"I'll get started right now," Maria said.

"I'll call you when supper's ready," Dad promised.

Journal:

How can you practice your faith today as you wait for Jesus to come again?

Pray:

Jesus, help me live as Your child in Your kingdom as I wait for the life eternal to come. Amen.

S. T.

Buried Treasure

The kingdom of heaven is like treasure hidden in a field, which a man found and covered up. Then in his joy he goes and sells all that he has and buys that field.

Matthew 13:44

Would you be excited if you found buried treasure? I know I would. I think most people would. If you could claim that treasure by giving away everything you have right now, would you make the trade? That might be a hard decision. With a new treasure, though, you probably could buy anything you wanted, even the things you have right now.

Jesus said the kingdom of God is like a man who found a buried treasure. Some people think Jesus meant we should be like that man. They say we should give everything to Jesus so we can be Christians, but that's not true. We did not become Christians this way. We did not find Jesus. He found us. We were buried in our own sins. Because of all the wrong things we have done, we do not look like treasure.

But Jesus says we are a treasure. He was willing to give everything He had for us. His friends ran away from Him. His enemies lied about Him. He was nailed to a cross. He suffered and died. He gave everything He had for one reason—so He could claim us as His treasure.

Of course, Jesus did not stay dead. He rose from the dead and lives forever. Because He died on the cross, we belong to Him. We are His treasure today and forever.

When you think about finding buried treasure, remember how Jesus feels about you. He gladly gave all He had, even His own life, to purchase you. You are His treasure.

Journal:

Draw and decorate a treasure chest with your name on it.

Pray:

Jesus, I am sorry that I don't always act like a treasure. Forgive me. Thank You for dying on the cross so I can belong to You forever. Amen.   S. T.

A Treasured Heirloom

Jasmine pulled the quilt tightly around her shoulders as the night air made her shiver.

"Grandma," she said, "I like sitting out here at night and watching the stars with you, but I get so cold. I'm thankful for this old quilt to wrap up in."

"Jasmine, that warm quilt is also very special."

"What's so special about this old thing?" Jasmine asked as she examined its faded patterns of red, blue, and green.

"It's special because my grandmother made it for me when I was a little girl. It is an heirloom quilt and has been passed down from one person to another in our family. Someday, I will give it to you because you are my heir."

Jasmine thought about Grandma's words for a few minutes before saying, "Wow, this is special! Not only does it keep me warm, but it also tells the story of how our family has loved and

He saved us, not because of works done by us in righteousness, but according to His own mercy, by the washing of regeneration and renewal of the Holy Spirit.

Titus 3:5

taken care of one another. When it is mine, Grandma, I am going to take good care of this quilt. Maybe someday I will have a child and will pass on my love and this quilt."

"Here's another thought, Jasmine. You are an heir to another gift, an even more valuable one."

"What gift is that?" asked Jasmine.

"When you were baptized," Grandma explained, "you became part of God's family of believers. Because Jesus paid for your sins, you are an heir to all that He won for you. Those gifts include forgiveness, life, and salvation." Then Grandma wrapped her arms around Jasmine and said, "You see, my dear, Jesus wraps you in His love. You are an heir and a child of heaven."

Journal:

What has someone passed on to you? What will Jesus give to you?

Pray:

Dear God, thank You for making me Your child and an heir of heaven through Jesus Christ. In His name I pray. Amen.   C. H.

The Lord will rescue me from every evil deed and bring me safely into His heavenly kingdom. To Him be the glory forever and ever. Amen.

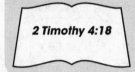

2 Timothy 4:18

A Rescue Hug

Darius was babysitting his little brother in the yard while their mom cooked spaghetti in the kitchen. He watched from the bottom of the stairs as his brother struggled to climb up the steps into their house.

"Jensen, be careful!" Darius shouted. "You're going to fall."

Two-year-old Jensen teetered back and forth, back and forth. Finally, he lost his balance and fell backward.

Darius moved quickly up the steps and caught Jensen before he could get hurt.

Jensen looked up at his older brother and fussed. "Why are you hugging me, Darius?"

Darius grinned and held on tightly. "I'm giving you a rescue hug, buddy," he replied.

Sometimes we doubt God; our faith is unsteady. We sin and teeter back and forth. Because of our sinful words, thoughts, and actions, we fall away from God. Boom! Down we go, unable to save ourselves.

But our God is in the saving business. He promises to rescue us from evil, from every evil. He promises to bring us safely into His heavenly kingdom.

God loved us so much that He sent His Son to die on the cross for us. Jesus allowed Himself to be arrested and tried for our sins. He stretched out His arms on the cross and died. But the soldiers couldn't defeat Him. The church rulers couldn't defeat Him. Not even death could defeat Him. On Easter morning, Jesus rose—so will you. End of rescue.

Journal:

When was a time that you needed to be rescued?

Pray:

Jesus, we thank You for loving us so much that You died on the cross to give us the rescue hug that saved us from all of our sins. Amen.   C. H.

Blowing in the Wind

Maria whispered, "Here she comes again."

She and Luisa watched the small bird return to the top of a fence rail. The girls were planning to take some video of the mother going in and out of the wind chime birdhouse. Still as stones, they waited with a camera.

The wren looked around for several seconds. An insect wiggled in her beak. The mother ducked into the top of the wind chime. After a bit, she emerged. Then off she went to find more food.

The little-girl statues listened to the tinkling of the wind chimes and waited for the right moment. They watched the mother bird fly in and out, feeding the young birds inside the birdhouse. Finally, Maria was able to take a video of the mother bird perched on the chimes.

A wind chime seems an odd place for a bird to build its nest and raise its young. Wind chimes are meant to be tossed about in the wind. That seems like a dangerous place for fragile eggs and baby birds. But inside, the mother bird had layered twigs, leaves, and grass into a tightly woven nest. Even though the wind chimes blew around, the baby birds were safe in the nest.

Everyone then who hears these words of Mine and does them will be like a wise man who built his house on the rock. And the rain fell, and the floods came, and the winds blew and beat on that house, but it did not fall, because it had been founded on the rock.

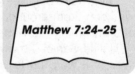

Matthew 7:24–25

Our homes can be like that wren's home. There are many spiritual winds that try to blow us around. There are bad messages on television. Whoosh! There are temptations on the Internet. Whoosh! Even our sinful nature wants to lie, cheat, and steal. Double whoosh!

In all this turmoil, God's children have a safe home. We are built on the rock of Jesus Christ and fed by His Word. We are baptized children of God, safe from the evil one. We are His, and He is ours.

Journal:

Write about a time God protected you from the dangers of this world.

Pray:

Dear Jesus, my Lord and Savior, thank You for being a solid rock in my life. Amen.   *C. H.*

JUNE
11
Tuesday

As far as the east is from the west, so far does He remove our transgressions from us.

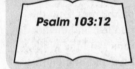

Psalm 103:12

Garbage Day

"Oh no! I overslept!"

Daniel jumped out of bed as soon as his eyes opened. It was garbage day, and he had not taken the garbage to the street. The sound of the truck coming down the street had awakened him.

Daniel dove into his jeans and pulled a T-shirt over his head. He slipped on his tennis shoes without stopping to tie them. He quickly ran to collect garbage from the wastebaskets around the house. Once he had all the garbage collected, he grabbed the two large garbage bags and headed for the street. The truck was already stopped in front of his house, loading garbage from his neighbor's house. He added his garbage and breathed a sigh of relief.

Returning to the house, Daniel was thankful he had removed the garbage from the house. If it had stayed around for another week, it would have become stinky.

Our sins fill our lives with garbage. While our sins are unpleasant when we keep them around, we just seem to add more and more sins to our already smelly hearts.

Unlike Daniel, however, we are powerless to remove the sin from our lives. If it were up to us, they would become smelly piles in which we wallow.

God did not leave it to us. He knew that taking the garbage of our sin out of our lives would be impossible for us, and so He sent His only Son, Jesus. Jesus removes our sins from our lives, creating clean hearts within us.

Journal:

What does it mean to you to know that Jesus has removed the garbage of sin from your heart?

Pray:

Dear Jesus, thank You for loving me so much that You removed all the garbage from my heart through Your death and resurrection. Amen.   *C. H.*

For I do not do the good
I want, but the evil I do
not want is what I keep
on doing.

Romans 7:19

Mule Jumping

"Watch this one, Anna! This is my favorite mule to watch!"

Anna looked on with excitement as the mule was brought into the staging area. The girl leading the mule was only about twelve years old. She led the mule into the pen, up to the bar that was five feet off the ground, and motioned for him to jump.

Anna held her breath as she watched. "Will he do it, Dad? Will he jump over the bar?"

"I don't know, Anna. Sometimes they choose to jump, and sometimes not."

The whole audience was quiet as they watched the young girl try to get the mule to jump. Nothing worked. The mule refused to jump. Finally, after several attempts, the girl led the mule out of the pen.

Mules are stubborn, strong animals. When mules decide to do or not do something, it is hard to convince them otherwise.

We are often like mules ourselves when it comes to sin. We know what God asks us to do and how He wants us to live, yet we still choose to continue in our sins.

God understands that we have a problem. We continue to do the wrong things, even when we want to do the right things. He knows we often sin, even when we want to do good. Because of His understanding of who we are and of His great love for us, He sent His only Son to make payment for the sins we continue to do. Jesus jumped the bar for us by dying on the cross.

Journal:

What is a time that you remained stubborn, even when you knew you were doing wrong?

Pray:

Jesus, I often hold on to my stubborn sin, even when I know the good I should be doing. Thank You for the forgiveness You offer me through Your death on the cross. Help me to live according to Your will. Amen.   C. H.

High Waters

Ekkk! Lana's mother slammed on the brakes of the car.

Lana and her mother were driving on a curvy road when they rounded a turn and saw a barricade blocking their way.

"Wow, that was a close one, Mom."

Looking at the barricade directly in front of them, Lana read the sign: "Impassable when high water present."

Beyond the barricade, Lana could see the dark, swirling waters of the creek as it crossed over the roadway. On the other side of the creek, Lana saw houses on hills, safely out of the flooded waters.

"Mom, look at those houses over there. How do those people leave their homes when the creek is so high?"

Following Lana's gaze, her mother said, "They have rowboats. When the water starts to get high, they park their cars on this side of the creek. When they need to go to work or school, they first row across the creek to their cars."

By faith the people crossed the Red Sea as on dry land, but the Egyptians, when they attempted to do the same, were drowned.

Hebrews 11:29

Lana was thoughtful. "It must be scary to cross the creek that way."

"I'm sure it is," answered Mom. "That makes me think about the Israelites when they crossed the Red Sea to flee from Egypt. They must have been very scared as they looked up at the walls of water towering above them."

"How could they do that, Mom? I would have been afraid to walk through that water!"

"They had faith that God loved them and would provide for them no matter how scary things looked."

Looking at the fast-moving creek on the other side of the barricade, Lana said, "It's great to have a powerful God when we face high water in life."

Journal:

Describe a time when you were called on to have faith in God.

Pray:

Dear God, help me to trust You during times of high waters. Amen.   C. H.

For God did not send His Son into the world to condemn the world, but in order that the world might be saved through Him.

John 3:17

Bored and Chored

Jake was bored. He didn't like being away from his friends while he spent summers with his dad. His mom had remarried, and he had two stepsisters at that home. At Dad's, he had more peace and quiet. But by the end of the week, he was missing the girls and his mom.

Jake was already tired of his video games. He used a set of codes he got from Christopher and beat his favorite game. He could go online for only an hour each day. He couldn't afford to buy more games, and he didn't want to do his chores.

His chores. That was another issue. Each day, his dad left a list of things to do. He was supposed to do dishes every morning with Hilary, his sister. Usually she slept late, and sometimes he ate lunch or had baseball practice before she ate breakfast. He was also supposed to read three books each week, but he didn't feel like it. He always put off practicing piano until the night before his lesson. He didn't want to clean his room either. Jake felt bad about not doing the chores; his dad looked disappointed with him.

Friday night, Jake's dad talked to him again about doing his chores. Jake's dad made it clear that he loved Jake regardless of the chores. It didn't mean Jake could ignore his chores, but his dad's love wasn't related to what Jake did right or even what he did wrong. Jake's dad loved him unconditionally.

God loves us unconditionally. He does not love us because we do chores quickly or perfectly. He loves us because of Jesus. Through Jesus, God has given us a new life in Baptism. And in that new life, we are able to do great things for others in His name.

Journal:

Write a list of chores and mark two that you like to do best. How do you serve God while doing them?

Pray:

God, thank You for loving me whether I do my chores or not. Give me a willing spirit to love and serve others. In Jesus' name I pray. Amen.   *J. G.*

Play and Pray

On Saturday, Jake got up early. He missed the sign-up deadline for the community baseball team, so his dad got him into a weekend tournament league. Every other Saturday, players would go to the park and be assigned to a team based on their practice stats. Because they never played on the same team more than once, the first couple of hours were spent getting organized and practicing.

Jake noticed that the shortstop on this team was wearing a Camp Concordia shirt. Jake didn't say anything at first, but he quickly learned that the shortstop's name was Kyle. After practice, while they were heading toward the field, Jake said, "I'm going to Camp Concordia tomorrow. Have you been there?"

Kyle said, "Really? I'm going there too! Cool."

Jake got four hits that first game. Kyle was a great infielder and one of the best hitters in the league. Kyle introduced Jake to one of Kyle's friends, Zach, on the other team. Zach and Kyle went to the Lutheran school together. Zach joked, "I prayed that we'd win all of our games today. I guess God is hearing my prayer."

Kyle said, "I prayed that too. I wonder whose prayer God will answer next." They laughed.

You may wonder how God chooses which prayers to answer yes and which He answers no or wait. God's answers are His way of giving us what is best for us. He invites us to ask Him things in prayer so we can receive His blessings, to seek things in prayer so we can find His grace, and to knock in prayer for doors to open.

Our greatest need is for salvation from sin, death, and the devil. God answered that need before we were ever born by giving us His Son, Jesus, who lived and died to pay for the sins of the whole world.

And I tell you, ask, and it will be given to you; seek, and you will find; knock, and it will be opened to you.

Luke 11:9

Journal:

Create a list of prayer requests, and then talk to God.

Pray:

Dear Jesus, forgive my selfish prayers and, through Your Spirit, guide me to pray for the most important things in my life. Amen.   J. G.

Have I not command-
ed you? Be strong and
courageous. Do not be
frightened, and do not
be dismayed, for the
LORD your God is with
you wherever you go.

Joshua 1:9

Beginnings

Jake had trouble sitting still in church. The hymns were some of his favorites, and the sermon had a good story that reminded him of God's love and care. But he kept checking his watch. After church, his dad was taking him and Hilary to lunch and then to Camp Concordia.

After a quick hamburger, they drove along the highway and then on back roads, following signs welcoming them to the camp. It was hilly and wooded, with farms dotting the roadside.

Finally, they pulled up to the camp. The parking lot was nearly full. Some kids and parents were unloading sleeping bags and suitcases, hauling them up to cabins that were surrounded by trees. A few girls were huddled in a circle near the main door of a building marked Dining Hall, and a few guys were playing catch.

Jake suddenly felt nervous. He realized he didn't know anyone here. He froze in the seat. His dad asked why he didn't want to go in. They talked for a while. His dad reminded Jake of how God promised to be with Joshua in the Bible and how He took away his nervousness. In Christ, we have confidence because Jesus has conquered everything for us. They prayed together. Then Jake saw Kyle, the shortstop from yesterday's game, unloading things from his car. Jake jumped out of the car and waved. Kyle didn't see him, but that was all it took. Jake had new energy. It was going to be okay with God on his side.

How about you? Do you ever suddenly feel nervous when you are about to do something new? God promises us in Baptism and in His Word that He is with us. Since Jesus died in our place and paid the way for us to be in God's family, God's name is on us. We belong to Him. New things aren't easy to do, but doing new things with God along can be exciting.

Journal:

List two things that make you nervous and how God helps you face them.

Pray:

Dear Jesus, give me peace when I become nervous, reminding me that You have conquered all of my fears. Amen.   *J. G.*

Statutes of Liberty

Have you ever been to the Statue of Liberty in New York Harbor? Isn't it wonderful? Even if you've never seen Lady Liberty in person, I'm guessing that you've seen photos of the robed lady holding a tablet in her left hand and raising high a torch in her right hand. The statue was a gift from France and arrived in sections on June 17, 1885. It weighs 450,000 pounds and stands over 305 feet tall. The official name of the statue is "Liberty Enlightening the World." When she was dedicated a little over a year later, President Grover Cleveland said, "We will not forget that Liberty has here made her home; nor shall her chosen altar be neglected."

Open my eyes, that I may behold wondrous things out of Your law. . . . Teach me, O LORD, the way of Your statutes; and I will keep it to the end.

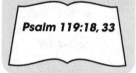

Psalm 119:18, 33

Thinking about the Statue of Liberty makes me think about God's statutes of liberty. Wait. What? Statutes of liberty? What does that mean? Well, when Moses was on Mount Sinai, God give him the Ten Commandments and many other rules and instructions, which we call statutes. Forty years later, when the children of Israel were about to enter the Promised Land, Moses reminded them to keep the commandments, rules, and statutes God had given them because God would love them and bless them (Deuteronomy 7:13).

But what do rules have to do with liberty? James calls God's Word the "law of liberty" (James 1:25). Why? Because in God's Law we see our sins, but in God's Word we see the righteousness that we have from Jesus' suffering, death, and resurrection. Jesus kept God's Law perfectly for us and set us free from sin, death, and the power of the devil! Praise God that His statutes of liberty have here made their home in our hearts, souls, and minds!

Journal:

Think about Lady Liberty's torch. How can her light remind us of God's light?

Pray:

"Teach me, O Lord, the way of Your statutes," and forgive me, in Jesus' name, when I fail to keep them. Amen. N. D.

And Peter said to them, "Repent and be baptized every one of you in the name of Jesus Christ for the forgiveness of your sins, and you will receive the gift of the Holy Spirit."

Acts 2:38

Baptism Birthdays

I'm so excited! Today is my Baptism birthday! Fifty-eight years ago today, my parents and godparents presented me to be baptized by our pastor in the name of the Father and of the Son and of the Holy Spirit. What a special occasion! But maybe you're wondering, what's the big deal? It's not like your real birthday, when you get cake and presents and maybe even a party, right? Well, you could have cake, presents, and a party. At my Lutheran school, we recognize Baptism birthdays in our chapel services. We don't have cake, but we do get a gift. This year, it was a seashell with our name on it.

But that's not why Baptism birthdays are so special. Jesus said, "Whoever believes and is baptized will be saved" (Mark 16:16). When He was about to ascend into heaven, Jesus also said, "Go therefore and make disciples of all nations, baptizing them" (Matthew 28:19). In fact, Baptism was so important to Jesus that even He was baptized! Can you imagine that? The sinless Son of God asked to be baptized, and He was! Why do You think He did that?

Martin Luther says that Jesus took all of our sins upon Himself and then drowned them in the waters of Baptism. That's why Baptism is so important: when we are baptized, we are marked with the cross of Christ and our sins are forgiven. Not only are our sins forgiven, but we also receive the gift of the Holy Spirit. And Paul says that when we are baptized, we "walk in newness of life" (Romans 6:4). What life? Eternal life! So, happy forgiveness-of-sins-Holy-Spirit-newness-of-life to me! Let the celebration begin!

Journal:

Why do you think that a seashell with three drops of water is a symbol for Baptism?

Pray:

Dear Jesus, thank You for the gift of Baptism and for the forgiveness of sins, the gift of the Holy Spirit, and the newness of life that I received in Your name. Amen.

N. D.

Little Blue

When I'm not teaching, one of my favorite things to do is to take photographs of birds, especially birds that you find along the shores of lakes, marshes, bays, and oceans. Two types of water birds I really like are herons and egrets. These water birds have long and slender toes, rounded wings, forward-facing eyes, short tails, and very sharp dagger-shaped bills so they can stab fish!

In and around the area where I live are many types of herons and egrets, and I have seen and photographed almost every one of them. The only one that I think I've never seen is the Little Blue Heron. Oops, did you catch that? You read that right: I think I've never seen one. Why am I not sure? Well, an adult is the only heron that is little and blue, and I've never seen one of those. But a juvenile Little Blue is not blue. It's white! And because it's white, it looks like another bird called a Snowy Egret. Now, I know for sure that I've seen and photographed Snowy Egrets. However, I wonder how many of those white birds were really Little Blues that hadn't transformed yet!

By this you know the Spirit of God: every spirit that confesses that Jesus Christ has come in the flesh is from God.

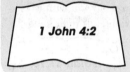

1 John 4:2

When Jesus gave His Sermon on the Mount, He warned His disciples to "beware of false prophets, who come to you in sheep's clothing but inwardly are ravenous wolves" (Matthew 7:15). What did Jesus mean? False prophets pretend to be followers of Jesus, but they are really trying to make Christians turn away from Jesus. They act like Jesus' sheep, but they are really dangerous wolves. That sounds just as tricky as the Little Blues! But don't worry. I can learn to recognize a juvenile Little Blue by looking at its bill. (It has a black-tipped bill!) And Jesus says that we can learn to recognize His prophets by their fruits—a true prophet of Jesus teaches that only Jesus is the way, the truth, and the life. God bless the true prophets!

Journal:

What is another name Jesus used for Himself? What does that name teach you about Jesus?

Pray:

Jesus, help me to always listen to Your voice. Forgive me when I go astray and lead me to the path that is higher than myself. Amen.   *N. D.*

Fear not, for I am with
you; be not dismayed,
for I am your God; I
will strengthen you,
I will help you, I will
uphold you with My
righteous right hand.

Isaiah 41:10

Fear Not!

What scares you? Spiders? Snakes? Thunderstorms? Roller coasters? When I was a kid, I was afraid of the dark. I have to admit, I still use a nightlight—mostly so I won't trip over my cat in the middle of the night, but I do like the light better than the dark!

In 1975, a movie came out that completely changed people's fears forever. Ever since that day, June 20, 1975, just the sound of the music in that movie scares folks: Da dah, da dah, da dah, da dah da dah da dah . . . ! Watch out! Have you guessed it? The movie was called *Jaws*, and almost everyone who has seen the movie is now afraid of sharks! Of course, the chance that you or anyone else will be killed by a shark is slim. In fact, according to the International Shark Attack File, the odds of being attacked and killed by a shark are one in 3.7 million. Phew! Feel better?

Another attack that we need not fear is Satan's. Peter wrote that the devil prowls around, trying to trick us, but we can resist him because of Jesus. Jesus loves us so much that He suffered, died, and rose again to keep us safe from the power of the devil. When we're scared, Jesus says to us, "Peace! Don't be afraid!" (see John 14:27). He also says, "Fear not, little flock, for it is Your Father's pleasure to give you the kingdom" (Luke 12:32). Phew! Feel better? I do! I pray that you do too.

Journal:

What scares you? How can you overcome your fear?

Pray:

Lord Jesus, whenever I'm afraid, please calm my fears with Your peace. Amen.   *N. D.*

Summer Solstice

Do you know what today is? It's the summer solstice! What does that mean? Well, if you're a scientist, it means that the North Pole is tilted toward the sun at a 23-degree angle. It also means that the sun will travel its longest path today, which causes our Northern Hemisphere to have more daylight than on any other day. But if you're a kid (or a teacher), it simply means today is the first day of SUMMER! Hooray! Of course, if you live in the Southern Hemisphere, today is the first day of winter, but that's a story for another science lesson!

From the rising of the sun to its setting, the name of the LORD is to be praised!

Psalm 113:3

So, how do you spend your summer days? Do you ride your bike, swim at the pool, or play at the park? Maybe you attend camp or Vacation Bible School. Does your family go on vacation? My family goes to the beach every summer. Other families travel to the mountains or go sightseeing. Some go to family reunions. No matter how we spend our time, almost everyone enjoys summer!

Did you know that there was a special day in the Bible when the sun stood still? After Joshua and the Israelites conquered Jericho and Ai, the people of Gibeon made peace with the Israelites. This worried the other five kings in the area, so they joined their armies together and set out to attack Gibeon. The Gibeonites were terrified! But Joshua called upon the Lord, and the Lord answered, "Do not fear them, for I have given them into your hands" (Joshua 10:8). Then God threw the enemy forces into a panic and struck them down with hailstones, and the sun stood still!

Our God surely is an awesome God! He creates the seasons for us to enjoy. He defeats all our enemies: sin, death, and the devil.

Journal:

Read Psalm 113:3. Think of a way you can praise God as you are enjoying your favorite summer activity.

Pray:

Dear God, thank You for all of the blessings of summer. Help me to honor You in all that I do each day of this season. In Jesus' name. Amen.   *N. D.*

Pass the Mustard

And He said, "With what can we compare the kingdom of God, or what parable shall we use for it? It is like a grain of mustard seed, which, when sown on the ground, is the smallest of all the seeds on earth, yet when it is sown it grows up and becomes larger than all the garden plants and puts out large branches, so that the birds of the air can make nests in its shade."

Mark 4:30–32

What foods do you like to eat in the summertime? Watermelon? Corn on the cob? Hot dogs and hamburgers? I love them all! What do you put on your hot dog? I like mustard and pickles. But there are others who use ketchup, cheese, onions, relish, or hot peppers. That made me wonder what the most popular hot dog topping really is. So, I did a little research, and the winner is . . . mustard! Seventy-one percent of Americans pick mustard as their favorite. In fact, we've been putting yellow mustard on our hot dogs since at least 1904! That's a long time!

You probably know that ketchup is made from tomatoes, and you may know that relish is chopped-up pickles. But do you know what mustard is? That yellow paste that we squirt onto our hot dogs and hamburgers is made from the seeds of mustard plants. The tiny seeds are ground up and then mixed with water, vinegar, or other liquids. Depending on the type of mustard, spices might be added, but the most basic mustard is just ground seeds and enough water to make a paste.

Mustard grows all around the world. Jesus even used mustard plants in two of His parables. In one of those parables, Jesus compared the kingdom of heaven to a mustard seed planted by a farmer. The seed was very tiny, but it grew into a plant large enough for birds to build nests in the branches! He told this parable to explain that God's kingdom began small, with Jesus' ministry, but it was about to grow amazingly large. Guess who the birds are? You are! Everyone who loves Jesus nests in the branches of God's kingdom!

Journal:

Draw a picture of yourself in God's branches.

Pray:

I love You, Jesus. Thank You for holding me in Your branches. Amen.   N. D.

Ouch!

Now that it's summertime, do you like to wear flip-flops? I used to wear them when I went to the beach, until last summer. Now I don't wear them anymore. Why? Because last summer at the beach, I broke my toe while wearing my flip-flops! I was pushing an empty wheelchair and accidentally walked right into the back of it. My poor bare toes hit the wheel. Ouch! Sounds painful, doesn't it?

By the time I got home a few hours later, my toe was so swollen and dark, it looked like a black olive! After an X-ray the next day, I found out that I had chipped the bone in my toe. It's called a hairline fracture, and it took a long time to heal. I was really glad when I could finally wear shoes and socks again. No more flip-fops for me!

For God so loved the world, that He gave His only Son, that whoever believes in Him should not perish but have eternal life.

John 3:16

When the serpent deceived Eve and Adam in the Garden of Eden, God punished them. But God also gave them a very special promise when He punished the serpent. "I will put enmity between you and the woman, and between your offspring and her offspring; He shall bruise your head and you shall bruise His heel" (Genesis 3:15). Ouch! Sounds painful, doesn't it?

What did God mean? This was His promise to Adam and Eve and to all of us—Satan would bruise Jesus, the offspring of Eve, on the cross. But then Jesus would crush Satan's head by conquering sin and death. Wow! That's really painful . . . to Satan! But it's a wonderful blessing for us. Jesus took our sins to the cross. He took the punishment we deserved. And then Jesus defeated sin, death, and the power of the devil when He rose from the grave. Wow! That's really wonderful—for us! Thank You, Jesus!

Journal:

Tell about a time when you were hurt. How did Jesus help you?

Pray:

Jesus, I praise and thank You for forgiving my sins and for Your promise of eternal life. In Your name I pray. Amen.   *N. D.*

[Jesus] told them this parable: "What man of you, having a hundred sheep, if he has lost one of them, does not leave the ninety-nine in the open country, and go after the one that is lost, until he finds it? And when he has found it, he lays it on his shoulders, rejoicing. And when he comes home, he calls together his friends and his neighbors, saying to them, 'Rejoice with me, for I have found my sheep that was lost.'"

Luke 15:3–6

No One Lost

Have you lost anything lately? Over an average person's lifetime, he or she will spend a year looking for lost objects. Some of the items we lose, such as a pencil or sock or soccer ball, may only inconvenience us. But some things, such as a house key, a cell phone, or a large sum of money, are expensive and even dangerous to lose. The worst loss of all is the loss of a person to sin and the devil.

We are Jesus' "sheep." Without faith in Him, we are lost in our sins. But Jesus, our Good Shepherd, died and rose to save us from our sins. He leads us to saving faith in Him. Jesus does this because He loves us. We are precious to Him. When a person is lost in sin, our loving Savior does not leave him or her. Instead, He looks for that individual. Jesus calls everyone to repent of their sins and to trust in His Gospel promise of forgiveness and eternal life through faith in Him. Even if you were the only one of Jesus' sheep to ever sin, He still would have suffered and died to save you. Jesus does not want anyone to be lost from Him.

Journal:

Write your first name. After it, write down two things you've lost and never found. Now, circle your name and draw a cross over it. Rejoice that through faith, you will never be lost from Jesus.

Pray:

Dear Jesus, thank You for rescuing me from my sins. Guide me and lead me so that I may never be lost from You. Amen. D. G.

[Jesus said,] "And if I go and prepare a place for you, I will come again and will take you to Myself, that where I am you may be also. And you know the way to where I am going." Thomas said to Him, "Lord, we do not know where You are going. How can we know the way?" Jesus said to him, "I am the way, and the truth, and the life. No one comes to the Father except through Me."

John 14:3–6

The Only Way

In 2018, twelve young soccer players and their coach were trapped in a flooded cave in northern Thailand for seventeen days following a hike. For days, rescuers frantically tried to find another entrance to release the trapped athletes. It was finally determined that the only way these boys and their coach could be saved was to have trained divers lead them out of the cave, one by one. To reach safety, each person had to be pulled through frigid waters along a two-and-a-half-mile path. Racing against rising floodwaters and plunging oxygen levels in the cave, it took divers three days to safely rescue all twelve boys and their coach.

We were once trapped in our sins. The only way we could be rescued from our sins was through Jesus, our Savior. Jesus suffered and died on the cross to pay the price we could not pay for our sins. When Jesus rose from the dead, He conquered the deadly grip that sin, death, and the devil have on us.

Jesus says, "No one comes to the Father except through Me." Jesus is the only way to salvation and eternal life. Through faith in Him, we receive forgiveness of sins, eternal life, and a home in heaven.

Journal:

How would you answer this question: What is the way to heaven?

Pray:

Dear Jesus, lead me to trust that faith in You is the only way to heaven. Help me to share this truth with others. Amen.   *D. G.*

Our Focus

Did you know that your eyes are always looking at your nose? The reason you don't see it is that your brain chooses not to focus on it. The scientific term for this is "unconscious selective attention." Scientists believe that because our brain considers the sight of our nose unimportant, it instead puts its attention on other things in our field of vision.

Today's Bible reading tells us we are to look to Jesus. From the time we are baptized, the Holy Spirit works in us to place and keep our focus on Jesus, who died and rose so that we might live. When we look to Jesus, we trust in His saving love and rely on His unmatched strength and power over all things.

Through faith in Jesus, we can "lay aside every weight, and sin which clings so closely" (Hebrews 12:1). Jesus tenderly invites us to lay our burdens on Him (Matthew 11:28). Our all-powerful Savior willingly relieves us of the burden of sin through His grace and forgiveness. We can give our worries and troubles over to Him and know that He will help us. Jesus promises to always be with us as He leads us to our heavenly home.

Therefore, since we are surrounded by so great a cloud of witnesses, let us also lay aside every weight, and sin which clings so closely, and let us run with endurance the race that is set before us, looking to Jesus, the founder and perfecter of our faith, who for the joy that was set before Him endured the cross, despising the shame, and is seated at the right hand of the throne of God.

Hebrews 12:1–2

Journal:

As you look to Jesus today, what sin or struggle might you lay aside?

Pray:

Lord Jesus, thank You for rescuing me from my sins. Lead me to lay aside all my sins and troubles as I remember that You have conquered them all. Help me to keep my focus on You and on Your good and gracious will for me. Amen.

D. G.

Do not be deceived, my beloved brothers. Every good gift and every perfect gift is from above, coming down from the Father of lights with whom there is no variation or shadow due to change.

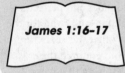

James 1:16–17

Upside Down or Right-Side Up

Whether you turn the numbers of the year 1961 upside down or right-side up, the numbers read the same. This will not happen again until the year 6009.

Illness, natural disasters, violence, struggles at home or at school, and our own sins can turn our lives upside down in an instant. Changes in our lives can make us uneasy or afraid. At such times, we may wonder whom we can trust or where we can turn for help.

Today's Bible reading says that no matter what twists and turns may happen to us, God does not change. That's reassuring! We can always trust in the fact that our heavenly Father loves us. We know that this is true because He sent His only Son, Jesus, to rescue us from sin, death, and the devil. If God would make such a sacrifice for us sinful, disobedient people, we can be certain that He is always on our side. We can trust that God will never leave us. No matter what upside-down explanations of how to get to heaven the world may offer, we can be sure that salvation is found only through faith in Him. We can be confident that "every good gift and every perfect gift" (v. 17) comes from Him. Let's give thanks and praise to our never-changing God!

Journal:

Knowing that God never changes, how can you face anything that changes around you?

Pray:

Heavenly Father, thank You for all Your good and perfect gifts You daily give me. Thank You especially for Your unchanging love and forgiveness for me for Jesus' sake. Amen.

D. G.

100 Percent

Sergey and Sasha Korolev are a father/daughter acrobatic duo. They have trained and performed together for over ten years. In many of their dangerous stunts, Sasha balances her head on the top of her father's head. As she does so, Sasha performs gymnastic moves or twirls a baton with her feet. Sometimes Sergey even walks up and down ladders as he balances his daughter. Before a performance on a television talent show, Sasha was asked, "Are you scared?" "No," she replied. "I trust my dad 100 percent."

When I am afraid, I put my trust in You. In God, whose word I praise, in God I trust; I shall not be afraid.

Psalm 56:3–4

In today's Bible reading, David expressed this kind of confidence in God, his heavenly Father. When pursued by enemies, David trusted in his heavenly Father's strength and power to help him. As he relied on God to keep him safe, David was no longer afraid. David trusted in God 100 percent.

We can trust in God our heavenly Father whenever we are afraid. God has already rescued us from our greatest enemies—sin, death, and the devil—through Jesus' death and resurrection. God's power and strength are greater than anything and anyone. When fears try to unbalance us, God keeps us steady. He always cares for us. Through faith in Him, we have nothing to fear. We can always trust in God 100 percent.

Journal:

Recall a dangerous situation you encountered. How did God bring you safely through it?

Pray:

Heavenly Father, You are stronger than anything and anyone! When I am afraid, help me trust in You. In the name of Jesus, who defeated sin, death, and the devil for all people, I pray. Amen.

D. G.

Oh, taste and see that the LORD is good! Blessed is the man who takes refuge in Him! Oh, fear the LORD, you His saints, for those who fear Him have no lack! The young lions want and hunger; but those who seek the LORD lack no good thing.

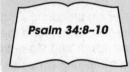

Psalm 34:8–10

Taste and See

"Grandma, what smells so good?" Bryce asked.

"It's peach pie," Grandma answered. "Would you like to taste it and see how good it is?"

"You don't have to ask me twice," Bryce eagerly replied.

Grandma placed a piece of the still-warm pie on a plate and set it in front of Bryce.

"This is delicious!" Bryce raved as he ate. "I can't wait to have more for dessert!"

God invites us to "taste and see" how good He is whenever we read or hear His Word and as we personally experience His goodness. God loves and cares for us as He provides for our needs through food, clothing, homes, and families. God protects us from evil and guards us from danger. God's greatest act of goodness for us was when He sent Jesus to rescue us from sin and eternal death. Through the faith we are given when we hear and read God's Word and when we are baptized, the Holy Spirit daily works in us to lead us to recognize and be thankful for all the good things that God our Father does for us.

Journal:

Write down three good things God has done for you today.

Pray:

Dear God, You have made everything, including me. Your goodness has no end. Thank You for all that You do every day to provide for all my needs, especially sending Jesus to be my Savior. Lead me into Your Word so that I may "taste and see" all of Your love and care for me. In Jesus' name I pray. Amen.

D. G.

A Weekly Family Reunion

Meghan was excited! Today she would gather with many of her relatives at their annual family reunion. Meghan could hardly wait to see her aunts, uncles, and cousins along with her grandparents and great-grandparents who traveled from many different places to gather together. Meghan loved these reunions. She especially enjoyed spending time with her family members who spanned several generations.

Worship at church with our brothers and sisters in Christ is a weekly family reunion we can all enjoy. In worship, we join with others in God's family of believers to joyfully sing praises to Him who made us, redeemed us, and constantly loves and cares for us. Gathered together, we thank God for making us members of His family through Holy Baptism. Gathered together, we listen to His true Word and are reminded that our sins are forgiven and that we have eternal life through faith in Jesus. Gathered together, we pray for the needs of others and rejoice in the goodness God gives to all. Our Christian family may span many generations. At worship, the Holy Spirit joins together young and old who share the same faith to celebrate our triune God's unending love.

Make a joyful noise to the LORD, all the earth! Serve the LORD with gladness! Come into His presence with singing! Know that the LORD, He is God! It is He who made us, and we are His; we are His people, and the sheep of His pasture. Enter His gates with thanksgiving, and His courts with praise! Give thanks to Him; bless His name! For the LORD is good; His steadfast love endures forever, and His faithfulness to all generations.

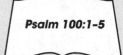

Psalm 100:1–5

Journal:

What is a particular joy God gives you as you worship Him together with your Christian family?

Pray:

O Lord, I love to sing praises to You. Thank You for making me a part of Your family of believers. May I continue to joyfully join with my Christian family to worship You. In Jesus' name I pray. Amen.   D. G.

June

Bible puzzles, games, and activities

Solutions on page 40

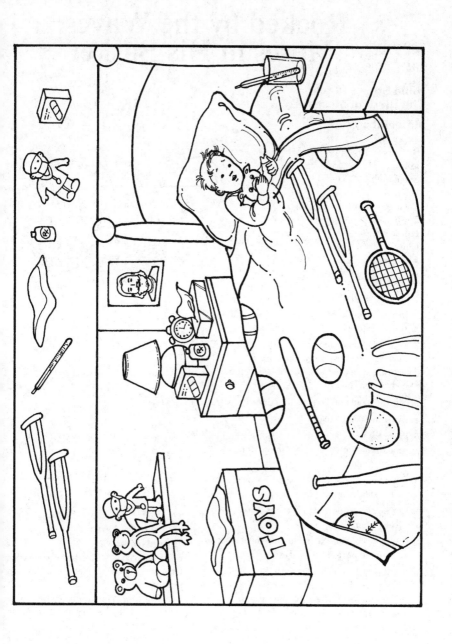

35

Rocked by the Waves: Moses in His Basket

Bible Story:
The Birth of Moses (Exodus 2:1–10)

Materials:
Paper plate
Scissors
Marker
Sponge
Dish
Tempera paint (orange or brown)
Toy block
Fabric scraps
Glue
Blue yarn

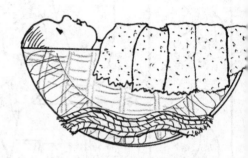

Directions:

1. Fold paper plate in half.

2. Draw a line 1½" below the folded edge of the plate for the top of the basket.

3. Using the illustration as a guide, outline Moses above the line you just drew, making sure that a part of the head and body touch the fold.

4. Cut the head and body as illustrated.

5. Draw in Moses' face.

6. Place the sponge in the dish. Pour a small amount of orange or brown tempera paint on the sponge.

7. Use the toy block to stamp paint over the outside of the paper plate. Let dry.

8. Cut fabric scraps and glue them on for Moses' blanket.

9. Cut pieces of blue yarn and glue them over the curved part of the basket for water.

10. Rock the plate back and forth. Pretend baby Moses is rocking in the river, waiting for Pharaoh's daughter to come and find him. Let the baby in the basket remind you that just as God took care of Moses long ago, He takes care of you today.

Suggestions:

1. Color the basket with crayons or markers.

2. Glue torn paper-bag pieces over the paper plate.

3. Use food coloring to dye macaroni pieces yellow and blue. Let dry and glue on for the basket and water.

4. Glue on vertical pieces of green yarn for bulrushes.

Are You a Good Steward?

How can we change this scene to help this family be better stewards of God's creation? List five things.

_____   _____

_____   _____

_____

My Coloring Page

June Journal

Puzzle 1 Answer

Are You a Good Steward?

How can we change this scene to help this family be better stewards of God's creation? List five things.

Here are some ideas: Move sprinkler to be on the lawn, not the driveway. Keep dog on a leash. Put bike away, getting it out of the street. Replace gas mower with electric or push model. Spend time with friends. Keep water in the bird bath for the birds. Fix the flat tire. Pick up the soda can. Recycle the soda can.

JULY

June–August 2019
Vol. 61, Issue No. 4

Daily Readings for Young Christians

Contributors to the July devotions:

Nicole Dreyer, Leah Kamrath,
Julie Riddle, Jon Schkade, Carolyn Sims

Edited by Mark S. Sengele

I have stored up Your word in my heart, that I might not sin against You. Blessed are You, O LORD; teach me Your statutes!

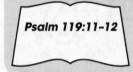

Psalm 119:11-12

Treasures

Corrie loved to go to the beach with her family. The quiet and peaceful coastline wasn't filled with swimmers and sunbathers. There, she could search for interesting shells and smooth pieces of driftwood.

While she was walking, a glitter in the sand caught her eye. She scooped up a pretty pink seashell, delighted with her find. A moment later, a second shell glittered at her. She gathered a green rock, two sticks, and a feather. Before long, Corrie's hands were so full of beach treasures she couldn't carry one more thing.

She looked ahead of her, down the beach. More interesting rocks and shells glinted at her from the sand. She smiled. When she came back, there would be more treasures to find.

Do you have a favorite Bible verse? Maybe there are some words that are meaningful to you or a verse that has helped you feel better. When you discover something special in the Bible, it's a treasure. You can scoop it up, enjoy it, and keep it in a special place to look at whenever you want.

But you know what? There are a lot of treasures in God's Word. Every time you visit it, you can see new precious words to store up and treasure. Words about Jesus, our rock. Words about the wood on which He died to give us life. Words about the water of Baptism, which makes us God's sons and daughters. Words that help you live a God-pleasing life. Words that bring you joy.

Ready to go on a treasure hunt? Grab your Bible and see what you find!

Journal:

What Bible verse is special to you? Why?

Pray:

Dear God, thanks for giving me Your Word. Help me remember to spend time reading my Bible, so that I can discover the treasures You have given me. Amen.

J. R.

Waiting

Today was the day. Lina bounced with excitement. "Mom, when will we go?"

Mom smiled. "For the twelfth time, Lina, we leave at nine o'clock. The animal shelter doesn't open until then."

Lina squeezed the rubber bone on the table. "I just can't wait to go pick up Buster. We finally get a dog!"

Lina had always wanted a dog. For ten years, she had looked at photos of dogs, drawn dog pictures, and dreamed about dogs. And now, finally, she was going to get the dog she'd wanted for so long. She was so happy she could almost burst.

"Mom, thanks for letting us get a dog," Lina said as she gave her mom a squeeze.

Her mom squeezed her back. "Well, you know what they say. Good things are worth waiting for. And speaking of good things . . . it's nine o'clock. Let's go get Buster!"

I tell you, there will be more joy in heaven over one sinner who repents than over ninety-nine righteous persons who need no repentance.

Luke 15:7

Have you ever had to wait for something you really, really wanted? How did you feel when you finally got that special thing? Pretty excited, right?

Did you know that angels get excited too? The Bible tells us that when even one person becomes a new child of God, the angels rejoice. And if the angels are happy, then God must be thrilled! What a joy it is to Him when He adds one more son or daughter to His family.

Because of Jesus, you are a part of God's family. And that means He is excited about you! On the day of your Baptism, on the day you became His child, He was truly happy. You were something worth waiting for.

Journal:

When have you waited for something special?

Pray:

Heavenly Father, thank You for making me a part of Your family through water and the Word. You are waiting for other people to join Your family. Help me to share Jesus' love with them. Amen.

J. R.

Feet

How beautiful upon the mountains are the feet of him who brings good news, . . . who brings good news of happiness, who publishes salvation, who says to Zion, "Your God reigns."

Isaiah 52:7

Look at your feet.

Seriously. Take a good look at your feet. If you're wearing shoes, take them off and take a peek at your piggies. It's okay, we'll wait until you're done. Go on. Look at your feet.

Well, did you look at them? What did you think? Were they small, fat, funny looking? Were they dirty? Is there sock fuzz between your toes? Do you have a blister on your heel?

Did you look down and say, "Wow! Those are some seriously beautiful feet"?

Feet are not beautiful, if you ask me. They can get pretty dirty, especially in summer. And they can even be a little bit stinky.

Now, if you were going to run around in the mountains, taking a message from one place to another, how do you think your feet would look? Not very clean, that's for sure.

So, what's so beautiful about these feet Isaiah's talking about? They are bringing good news. And what's the good news that they carry? It's that Jesus is our Savior. It's the news that God's in charge and mighty. They bring the news that God loves us enough to take care of us all the time and that we are never, ever alone.

Feet may be funny looking, but they can do amazing things. They can carry God's good news to us. And they can carry us to others, so that they can hear the good news too.

Journal:

Where will your feet carry you today? How can you share some good news there?

Pray:

Jesus, help me to be Your beautiful feet today! Amen.   *J. R.*

Blink!

Scotty and his family had just returned from their special picnic and were waiting for fireworks. He was kneeling in the front yard, gazing intently into the grass. Suddenly, he gave a little jump. "Mom!" he called. "Come see this!" He looked up at her with wonder in his eyes. "He's blinking!"

Mom looked where Scotty was pointing. There, crawling on a long blade of grass, was a slender black insect. It spread its thin wings wide and rose softly into the air just above their heads. Then the bug blinked. For just a moment, its underside lit up with a warm, cheerful light.

Scotty was delighted. "Mom, I didn't know bugs could do that!"

She laughed quietly and sat down beside him. "Not all insects can. But God made lightning bugs special." The insect blinked again. More blinks told them other fireflies were nearby.

In the same way, let your light shine before others, so that they may see your good works and give glory to your Father who is in heaven.

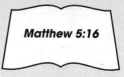

Matthew 5:16

"Mom," Scotty said softly, "I wish I were like a lightning bug."

"Why, sweetie?"

"They're so special. And they can go blink, blink, blink, and they light up the sky. They remind everyone how neat God is because He made such a neat bug."

"Oh, Scotty. You are a neat little bug!" she cried. "God made you to be just the way you are. He wanted you to blink—blink for other people just by being your terrific self. When they look at you and see how happy Jesus' love makes you, they can remember that He loves them and died for them too."

Scotty hopped up and began to zoom around the yard. "Look, Mom! I'm a lightning bug!" He stopped suddenly and turned to her. "Jesus loves you, Mom. Blink!"

Journal:

How can you "blink" in someone else's life today?

Pray:

Heavenly Father, thank You for sending Jesus to bring me light by dying on the cross for me. Help me to share Your light with others. Amen.   J. R.

Therefore, we are ambassadors for Christ, God making His appeal through us. We implore you on behalf of Christ, be reconciled to God.

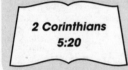

2 Corinthians 5:20

The Middle

Selah sighed. Her mother looked up from the sink. "What's wrong, darlin'?"

Selah gave her cereal a poke and then put her chin in her hand. "Brittany and Brianna are fighting. They both want me to take their side. I'm stuck in the middle again!"

"Hmm." Mom rinsed a soapy plate. "What do you think you might do?"

"The usual," Selah said. "They'll complain, I'll listen, I'll help them, and then they'll be friends again. Why do I always have to be the one who fixes all their arguments?"

Mom smiled. "'Blessed are the peacemakers,' dear" (Matthew 5:9). When Selah looked confused, Mom went on. "You're a peacemaker. I'm sure you get tired of always being the one in the middle." Selah nodded and sighed again. "But you're a real blessing to your friends. You know, Jesus was a peacemaker too."

"Because He helped people get along with each other?" Selah asked.

"Actually, no. The peace Jesus made was between God and us. We mess up a lot. But because Jesus died for us and rose again, God still loves us. It wasn't easy for Jesus to be in the middle either. But He did it for us because . . . ?"

Selah carried her bowl to the sink. "Because He loves us. And because He's our friend! Thanks, Mom. Gotta get ready to be in the middle." She put her fists on her hips and stood up straight, in her best superhero pose. "Just call me . . . the peacemaker!"

Journal:

How can you be a peacemaker for your friends today?

Pray:

Dear God, thank You for the peacemakers in my life. Thank You for sending Jesus, so that I can be at peace with You. Help me to share Your peace with others. Amen.

J. R.

Look to the Rock

Abigail looked down from the observation tower. "That," she said, "is one big hole in the ground."

She and her family were visiting a limestone quarry, the biggest one in the world. Looking far to the other side, Abigail could see water as endless as an ocean with ships sailing by.

Her cousin Nathan nudged her out of the way. "I can't believe how big this is. It's awesome!"

They read a sign explaining that a special kind of rock was taken out of the quarry, loaded on ships, and carried away to be used in making steel, cement, and chemicals. "Think of it!" Nathan said. "All over the country, there's stuff that's made using rock that came from right here, from out of this hole. It's like all that stuff is connected, and this is its real home."

Abigail poked him. "Pretty cool, Nathan. Not bad for a big hole in the ground!"

Listen to Me, you who pursue righteousness, you who seek the LORD: look to the rock from which you were hewn, and to the quarry from which you were dug.

Isaiah 51:1

There are rocks everywhere. The rocks that come from one particular quarry have something in common. Even though they're different and are used in different ways, they're all a piece of the same rocky area.

There are people everywhere, all special, all unique. But the people of God have something in common. God chose us to be a part of Jesus' family. We did not choose Him.

When you doubt that you are valuable, look to God. He chose you in Jesus Christ to be His child. He sends you off here and there with His forgiveness, power, and blessing. He helps you live in loving service to others.

Journal:

If people say they did good things to get into God's family, tell why they would be wrong. Explain who did the good and perfect thing.

Pray:

Dear God, thank You for choosing me and making me a part of Your family. I am honored that You would call me Your child. Amen.   *J. R.*

All Scripture is breathed out by God and profitable for teaching, for reproof, for correction, and for training in righteousness, that the man of God may be complete, equipped for every good work.

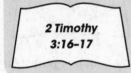

**2 Timothy
3:16–17**

Prepared

"Flashlight?" Check. "Bug spray?" Check. "Sleeping bag, hiking boots, marshmallows?" Check, check, check!

Griffin and his dad were going camping. They had been preparing all week for their trip, and Griffin wasn't sure he could wait much longer. "Dad, we've got enough stuff. Can't we just go?"

Dad made another check mark on his list. "Almost, Griff. I need to make sure we've got everything we need. Did you pack your hat?"

"It's on my head, Dad. Let's go!"

"Here's the map and the first-aid kit and the magnifying glass. Okay, kiddo. We've got it all. We're ready to go."

Griffin climbed in the car and buckled up. "With all this stuff, Dad, we're ready for anything!"

Camping trips, piano recitals, and social study tests all take preparation. So do the spiritual things in life. Do you know God prepares us for these things? He's given us His Word, the Bible.

God uses the Bible to get us ready to do the things He has in store for us to do. The more time we spend with it, the more prepared we are to face challenges we meet. God's Word comforts us, strengthens us, and gives us peace. He gets us ready to help others and to share the story of Jesus' love with them. His Word completes and equips us for every good work.

Jesus was prepared to do what He was born to do—die on the cross for our sins. Through the Word, God has given us faith in Him. Now, we have the joy of spending time in His Word, being strengthened in faith and prepared for a life spent serving others in His name.

Journal:

Do you have a favorite Bible verse? How might it prepare you for something you will face tomorrow?

Pray:

Dear Jesus, thank You for being ready to give Your life for me. Help me to be ready to share Your Word with my friends. Amen.   J. R.

Relax

Relax. That's what Gillian's teacher said, but Gillian held on to her with a iron grip. The teacher said she could trust the water to hold her up, but how could that be possible?

Still, Gillian really did want to learn to swim. All her friends loved the water, and she wanted to be a part of their summer fun. The Sunday School swim party was just a week away. Was it possible she could learn to relax and stay afloat?

Gillian decided to give it one more try. This time, instead of thrashing around and fighting the water, she took a deep breath. She let go of her teacher. She laid back her head. Can you guess what happened? Right. Gillian found herself being supported by the water—just as her teacher had promised.

"Be still, and know that I am God. I will be exalted among the nations, I will be exalted in the earth!" The LORD of hosts is with us; the God of Jacob is our fortress.

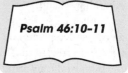

Psalm 46:10-11

In the Bible, God tells us to relax—to be still. That means instead of being afraid, we can trust God to help us. We can be still and know that our God is with us. We can count on Him. We can relax.

The most important thing God does for us is take away our sins. We could never do that by ourselves. But we can be still and know that God has forgiven us for Jesus' sake and made us His children.

Whenever you are afraid, remember that God is in control. Remember that He loves you. You can relax knowing you are in His care.

Journal:

Make a list of things you are afraid of. Pray for God to help you face these fears, to relax, and to do what you need to do. Then write how God answered your prayers.

Pray:

Dear God, thank You for loving me and taking care of me. Please help me relax because I know You are God and I can trust You for all things. For Jesus' sake I pray. Amen.

C. S.

9

Tuesday

He put another parable before them, saying, "The kingdom of heaven is like a grain of mustard seed that a man took and sowed in his field. It is the smallest of all seeds, but when it has grown it is larger than all the garden plants and becomes a tree, so that the birds of the air come and make nests in its branches."

Matthew 13:31–32

Small but Important

Prepare to go on a scavenger hunt. In the boxes below are names of things God created. Find as many as you can and either glue them into the squares or draw a picture of them. Most are very small but also very beautiful. If you are able to examine them with a magnifying glass, you will see even more of the beauty God created in them. In the blank boxes, place other discoveries you find.

Feather	Shell	Seed	Flower petal
Grass	Pebble	Thorn	Splinter

The items you found may look very small, but God can do important things with them. In today's Bible reading, He reminds us that tall trees begin as tiny seeds.

Our faith may start small too, but the Holy Spirit makes it grow as we read the Bible, go to church and Sunday School, share family devotions, and ask questions about God and His love.

Some people think children are too small to be important. But God thinks differently. He says children can have the best faith of all. No one is too small for Jesus to love enough to die for.

Journal:

Write about ways the items in your chart are important. Think about people you know whom God uses to do important things. What can you do to show your love for God and to help others?

Pray:

Dear Jesus, thank You for loving me and taking away my sins so I can be Your child and serve in Your kingdom. Amen.   C. S.

Beautiful Feet

How many pairs of shoes do you own? Go count them! Be sure to count slippers and flip-flops and cleats. Do you have three? six? ten or more?

Shoes are something we take for granted, but some children do not own even one pair of shoes. When McKenzie heard about children who couldn't go to school because they had no shoes to wear, she decided to do something about it.

She asked her classmates and all her friends and all her mother's friends to donate shoes to help those who had none. In two months, McKenzie collected 504 pairs of shoes! She gave them to children in need of them in the name of Jesus.

How are they to preach unless they are sent? As it is written, "How beautiful are the feet of those who preach the good news!"

Romans 10:15

Shoes can make your feet look beautiful. In Bible times, messages traveled as people moved about on feet. Paul traveled thousands of miles to take the Good News many places, often traveling by foot. That's why he says that those who share the Gospel have beautiful feet.

McKenzie used her feet to take her places where she could help others. She shared the Good News about Jesus by sharing His love.

The best news about Jesus is that He obeyed His Father's will and walked up to Calvary. There, His feet were nailed to the cross. There, He died to take away our sins. But Jesus didn't stay dead. He rose on Easter morning. McKenzie knew this Good News, and it made her want to help others too.

When we see people in need, we can help them in Jesus' name. They may not need shoes, but they may need a friend to talk to or a kind word or a reminder of God's forgiveness. When you help them, your feet are beautiful too.

Journal:

Make a list of clothing and shoes you have outgrown. Then donate them.

Pray:

Dear Jesus, thank You for giving me so much—not only shoes and clothes and toys, but also Your love and forgiveness. Please let me share my blessings with others in Your name. Amen.

C. S.

JULY

11

. . . .
Thursday
. . . .

"O death, where is your victory? O death, where is your sting?" The sting of death is sin, and the power of sin is the law. But thanks be to God, who gives us the victory through our Lord Jesus Christ.

1 Corinthians 15:55–57

Ouch!

Mia was enjoying the soft grass beneath her toes when suddenly she felt a sharp pain. Ouch! Ouch! Ouch! Mia hobbled into her house to take a closer look. That's when she discovered the black barb under her toe.

Mia had stepped on a bee! The bee left something behind in her foot—its poison sac and stinger.

Mom carefully scraped the stinger away so she wouldn't squeeze the sac and inject even more of the bee's poison into the wound, but the damage had already been done. Mom made a paste with baking soda. It helped for a while, but Mia's toe still hurt and itched. It took days for the swelling to go away.

When a bee attacks, it sticks its stinger into a person's skin. The stinger has a little hook on it so the bee can't pull it out again without tearing the stinger away from its body. The bee may sting to protect itself, but it cannot survive the sting.

Jesus stung the devil when He went to the cross. He won the victory and took away the devil's power over us. But in order to do that, Jesus had to die in the process. He gave up His life to protect us. The Good News is that, unlike a bee, Jesus didn't stay dead. He rose again on Easter Sunday. Now it is death that has lost its sting—forever.

Most bees don't want to hurt us, but if you are ever stung, remember how Jesus gave His life for you so that you can live forever.

Journal:

Find a picture of a bee in a book or on a website (with an adult's permission). Draw the stinger and poison sac. Draw a cross under your picture to remind you that Jesus gave His life for you.

Pray:

Dear Jesus, You gave up Your life to take away the sting of death. Thank You for giving me life forever with You in heaven. Amen.   C. S.

Properly Clothed

Manuel and his family drove all night and all day. Dad wanted to get as far along the road as possible before they had to stop for a good night's sleep. By the time they reached their first hotel, they had traveled almost nine hundred miles! Dad could hardly wait for a shower and a soft bed.

But when he went to unpack his pajamas, he couldn't find his suitcase. "Who loaded my suitcase in the trunk?" he asked.

Mom, Manuel, and Manuel's sister, Angela, looked at one another with blank stares. They each thought someone else had done it!

What could Dad do? It was too far to drive all the way back home. So he had to buy new clothes to wear.

The clothing Jesus was talking about in today's Scripture reading was a very special garment. The wedding host provided it for his guests so they could cover their own old clothes and wear a clean, new outfit in honor of him and of the occasion. It was an insult not to wear what the host provided.

Then he said to his servants, "The wedding feast is ready, but those invited were not worthy. . . . For many are called, but few are chosen."

Matthew 22:8, 14

What will we need to wear in heaven? Does God have a dress code? Actually, He does. We need to be clothed in the white robe of Jesus' righteousness. That means our sins are forgiven; we are clean and pure in God's sight. We can't buy this special clothing ourselves. God puts it on us when we are baptized—when the Holy Spirit puts faith in our hearts. We never outgrow this robe, and it never wears out. It is ours to put on every day of our lives.

Journal:

Describe or draw a picture of your favorite piece of clothing. Is it a sports jersey or a special dress? Tell why it is so special to you. Color over the picture with a white crayon as a reminder that Jesus covers our sins.

Pray:

Dear Jesus, thank You for clothing me in Your perfect righteousness. Please continue to forgive my sins so I am pure in Your sight. Amen.   C. S.

Or what woman, having ten silver coins, if she loses one coin, does not light a lamp and sweep the house and seek diligently until she finds it? And when she has found it, she calls together her friends and neighbors, saying, "Rejoice with me, for I have found the coin that I had lost."

Luke 15:8-9

Lost

Marina knew she should have obeyed her mother and left her new ring at home. It was a gift from her grandma, and Marina wanted to show it off to all her friends that day at the beach.

But when Marina put on sunblock, her fingers got slippery. A bit later, when she looked down at her hand, her new ring was gone! She frantically looked for it in the sand, but the search seemed hopeless.

Marina sobbed. She thought she would never see her beloved ring again.

Then a lifeguard truck came by. "What's wrong?" asked the lifeguard. "Are you hurt?" Marina explained what had happened.

"No problem," said the lifeguard, as he pulled a strange-looking device out of his truck. It looked like a plate on a stick. "This is my metal detector," he said. "It will beep when it senses metal in the sand, so we'll know right where to dig."

The lifeguard passed the metal detector over the sand in the area when Marina had been sitting. Suddenly, the detector beeped. With a little digging, Marina found the ring just beneath the surface. She was so excited, she jumped for joy.

We all know a lost ring cannot save itself. It's helpless; it's hopeless. But did you know we, too, are lost? We are lost in sin, and we cannot save ourselves. Like Marina who loved her ring and helped the lifeguard search for it, we need someone to love us and search for us. Jesus did that. In Luke 15, He tells us that He came to seek and save the lost. He came to give His life to redeem sinners.

What happens when lost rings are found? Someone is happy. What happens when sinners repent? Jesus says, "There is joy before the angels of God" (Luke 15:10). Now that is some kind of joy.

Journal:

Write about something you lost and then found. How did you feel?

Pray:

Dear Jesus, thank You for never giving up on me. Please keep me close to You forever. Amen.

C. S.

Living with Jesus

Michaela was excited. She was old enough to spend a month with her grandma in California. California was a long way from Virginia, where Michaela lived, but she wasn't afraid.

She would have to take an airplane all the way across the United States. She would have to be away from her mom and dad. She would have to leave her Virginia friends behind. But all those things were not a problem. Why?

Michaela would be with her grandma, who loved her. Michaela trusted Grandma to take good care of her. She thought about all the fun and exciting things she and Grandma would do. They would go to the beach. They would bake cookies. They would go to museums and maybe even an amusement park. But the best thing wasn't what they would do or where they would go. The best thing was that they would be together.

For God so loved the world, that He gave His only Son, that whoever believes in Him should not perish but have eternal life.

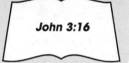

John 3:16

Someday, we will go on a trip to heaven. The Bible doesn't tell us all the things we will do in heaven, but we know that heaven will be a wonderful place. There will be happiness and no more tears. We will live there forever with Jesus, who died and rose so we can come in.

He loves us even more than our moms and dads and grandmas and grandpas. He takes better care of us than anyone else ever could. What an adventure heaven will be!

It will probably be many years before we go to heaven, but whenever you are having a great time with someone you love, think about the eternity you will spend with Jesus.

Journal:

Draw a picture of what you think heaven will look like. Be sure to include yourself and Jesus in the picture.

Pray:

Dear Jesus, thank You for the promise that I will live in heaven with You. You made that possible because You died on the cross to take away my sins. I love You because of Your great love for me. Amen.

C. S.

He Himself bore our sins in His body on the tree, that we might die to sin and live to righteousness. By His wounds you have been healed.

1 Peter 2:24

Special Stripes

"Mimi, look at my new zebra book. Isn't it neat?" said Brooke.

Brooke's grandmother gave her a hug. They sat down at the kitchen table and opened the book to take a look. "Tell me all about zebras, Brooke."

"Zebras live in Africa, and they run really fast, sometimes forty miles per hour! Zebras like to eat grass, and they need lots and lots of water. Oh, and they weigh over five hundred pounds!"

"Gracious!" exclaimed Mimi. "That's a lot of zebra!"

"My book also shows that zebras are black with white stripes. The stripes help protect zebras from becoming another animal's dinner, because it's hard to follow the stripes when zebras run. Zebras usually aren't bitten by tsetse flies because the stripes confuse the flies!"

"My goodness! I didn't know that!" Mimi said. "But I do know that no two zebras look alike. Every zebra's stripes are completely different from every other zebra—just like our fingerprints. The stripes make the zebra special."

God gave His creature the zebra stripes for a purpose. Jesus, God's Son, received stripes as part of God's purpose. On the night that Jesus was arrested and tried, He was whipped by soldiers. The whip left striped wounds on His back. Jesus suffered and died for our sins so that we might be healed of our sins. Now our sins are forgiven, and we can live with Jesus forever. That means Jesus' stripes are extra special.

Journal:

How did God create you to be special?

Pray:

Dear God, thank You for zebras and for the special ways You designed Your creation. Thank You for Jesus' stripes, which healed me from sin, giving me forgiveness and eternal life. In His name I pray. Amen. N. D.

Jesus Christ is the same yesterday and today and forever.

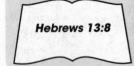

Hebrews 13:8

The Same, but Different

"Ashley! Sam! Kia! Time for Vacation Bible School."

"I can't wait to learn the new songs!" said Sam at breakfast.

"What's this year's theme?" asked Ashley.

Kia said, "I hope we do the camel walk like last year!"

"Don't be silly," Sam laughed. "VBS is different every year."

"It would be boring if we did the same thing every year," Ashley added.

"VBS is never boring!" Kia exclaimed. "I love it!"

Just then, Mom came with blueberry pancakes. "You're right. VBS is never boring, but you're wrong too. It is the same every year."

All three children looked at Mom. "No way!" "Are you sure?" "Huh?"

"Think about it," Mom said. "What do you learn in VBS?"

"We do different crafts," said Ashley.

"We sing new songs," said Sam.

"We eat silly snacks," said Kia.

"Yes, but that's what you do. Now tell me what you learn."

All three children thought and then started to smile. "We learn about Jesus!" they said.

"I like hearing about when Jesus was a baby," added Kia.

Sam said, "I like reading about Jesus' miracles."

"My favorite lesson is Jesus' resurrection," said Ashley.

"VBS changes every year," Mom explained, "but the message is the same: Jesus died on the cross and rose again to forgive your sins and give you a home in heaven. All of the crafts, songs, and even the snacks remind us of that message. Now, who's ready to go?"

"We are!"

Journal:

What is your favorite part of VBS?

Pray:

Thank You, Jesus, for VBS, so that I can learn more about how much You love me. Help us bring others to hear about You too. Amen.   *N. D.*

God's Shadow

When I was younger, my friends and I loved to play hide-and-seek. Sometimes in the summer, we were allowed to play in the dark. One night, I found the best place to hide. It was out in the open where the light from my parents' patio created a shadow at the bottom of the hill. Standing there, I was nearly invisible. My friends ran right by me. They couldn't see me. I was hidden in the shadow. What a safe place!

In the Old Testament, Isaiah the prophet warned the people of Judah that their sins would bring them great punishment. But Isaiah also reminded the people of how much God loved them. Not only would God redeem His people from their Babylonian captivity, but He would also send a Redeemer to save His people, all of His people, from their sins. Through Isaiah, God said, "[I have] covered you in the shadow of My hand. . . . 'You are My people'" (Isaiah 51:16). What a safe place!

> He who dwells in the shelter of the Most High will abide in the shadow of the Almighty.
>
> *Psalm 91:1*

King David also wrote about how much God loves His people. When David was afraid, he prayed, "I call upon You, for You will answer me, O God. . . . Hide me in the shadow of Your wings" (Psalm 17:6, 8). When David was rejoicing, he proclaimed, "How precious is Your steadfast love, O God! The children of mankind take refuge in the shadow of Your wings" (Psalm 36:7). What a safe place!

A priest in God's temple reminded everyone that when they worshiped God, they were living "in the shadow of the Almighty" (Psalm 91:1). What a safe place!

God loves us with an everlasting love. He has redeemed us through His Son, Jesus. Whenever we are playing with our friends or telling God that we are afraid or that we are sorry or thanking God for His blessings or worshiping in His house, we are safely hidden in His shadow. What a safe place!

Journal:

Write about a time when God protected you, when you were in God's shadow.

Pray:

Dear God, thank You for keeping me near You, safely in Your shadow. In Jesus' name I pray. Amen.   N. D.

My son, keep your father's commandment, and forsake not your mother's teaching. Bind them on your heart always; tie them around your neck. When you walk, they will lead you; when you lie down, they will watch over you; and when you awake, they will talk with you.

Proverbs 6:20–22

My Mother Told Me

Have you ever ignored something your mom told you to do? How often? I always tried to obey, but "clean your room" was a tough one for me.

Do any of these mom sayings sound familiar?

"Do your homework first."

"Don't throw things inside."

"Quiet down."

"Don't hit your brother."

There are hundreds more. Moms have a tough job just being moms. They're responsible for teaching their kids, feeding them, cleaning up, and making sure everything runs smoothly. Moms don't get a lot of thanks for it. One way to say thank you is by listening to and obeying them. It's a good idea anyway. Moms usually know what's best for you.

What your mother and father tell you to do is important. But what God tells you to do matters much, much more. God the Father knows more than your mom or dad ever could.

He also loves you with a love that—almost unbelievably—is greater than the love of parents or grandparents. He loves you so much that He sacrificed His own Son for you.

God knows what's best for you all the time. Even when you don't obey, He still offers forgiveness. He's still ready with the next word of advice and love.

Journal:

When is it hardest to obey your parents? How can you work on that?

Pray:

Father, since You know what's best for me, help me to listen and obey. Amen.

J. S.

To

Early Christmas morning, Selena didn't see a beautiful circle of presents around the tree. Instead, one jumbled pile of presents rested by the wall, while another pile was neatly stacked.

Her brother, Morgan, tossed another present.

"What are you doing?" called Selena.

"Organizing," said Morgan. "The bad ones go there." He pointed at the messy pile.

"And the good ones?" Selena asked.

He smiled. "The good ones say, 'To: Morgan.'"

I get how Morgan felt. My favorite word on any present or Valentine is the one after "To." When it says, "To: Jonathan," I know it's for me. The "To" matters because it lets us know the present isn't just for anyone. It's specifically for the person whose name comes after "To."

Many of the New Testament's writings are addressed to certain groups of people. Paul even wrote a couple to one young pastor named Timothy. Today's Bible reading, though, has a different sort of "To." You could say this book is addressed to us, to all Christians.

Jude, a servant of Jesus Christ and brother of James, To those who are called, beloved in God the Father and kept for Jesus Christ: May mercy, peace, and love be multiplied to you.

Jude 1-2

When it comes to the Bible's message, God addresses it to an even bigger "To." It's to all people. God wants everyone to know that His Son died on the cross to save them, and this salvation comes through faith. This message is a gift for everyone on earth. But, wonderfully, while it's for all people, it's also specifically for you.

Journal:

Whose day can you brighten by sending a message or gift just for them?

Pray:

God, You sent Your Son for me and gave faith to me. Thank You for making me Yours. Amen.

J. S.

No longer do I call you servants, for the servant does not know what his master is doing; but I have called you friends, for all that I have heard from My Father I have made known to you. You did not choose Me, but I chose you and appointed you that you should go and bear fruit and that your fruit should abide, so that whatever you ask the Father in My name, He may give it to you. These things I command you, so that you will love one another.

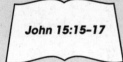

John 15:15–17

Pick

Imagine three lunches on the kitchen table. Which do you pick?

1. Peanut butter and jelly sandwich, apple, chips, and a brownie

2. Chicken nuggets, an orange, carrots, and a cookie

3. Sardines, brown lettuce, and broccoli pudding

If you had to pick second, you wouldn't be as happy. But what if you had to pick last? Most people would probably choose to skip lunch. Of course, food isn't the only thing we pick.

Whether it's for a team at recess or a birthday invitation list, we all want to be picked first. Sometimes, we want it even more if we know we don't deserve it. And have you ever been the one picking? The first choice can be obvious. But other times—like if you have two best friends—it's not easy.

It's harder when someone else has all the power. We don't want them to pick for us or, even worse, to not pick us at all. We don't need to be worried about that with God. While the power isn't in our hands, God chooses us to love and protect and forgive. He chooses us to receive the gift of faith, of believing in Him.

God put this faith in our hearts through Baptism and His Word. Because of this faith, we bear fruit—godly words and actions—that show His love to others.

Journal:

Do you know someone who's often picked last? How can you reach out to that person?

Pray:

Dear God, thank You for choosing me to be Yours. Help me to share Your love. Amen.

J. S.

The Very Best One

The science fair was packed. In just a few minutes, they'd announce the winners.

"You're going down," said Shantee.

"Nuh-uh," said Cherise. "First place is all mine."

"You're dreaming," said Shantee. "My spectrum analyzer beats whatever that is by a mile."

Cherise smirked. "Yours might get second place, but my project is the best."

Strongest. Fastest. Smartest. Greatest Watermelon Seed Spitter Ever. There's nothing like being amazing at something. It's even better if everyone else knows you're better than they are.

More than once, Jesus' disciples argued about who was the greatest. You'd think being Jesus' closest chosen followers would be enough for them. They all got to speak with Jesus, to learn from Him. They all shared food and drink and daily life with the Messiah. But they wanted more. They wanted to be the greatest of the Twelve, the greatest of all in God's kingdom. So they argued.

But Jesus defines greatness differently. As God's Son, He is literally the greatest man to ever live. But did He brag about it or use it to make others feel bad? No. Jesus shared a true sign of greatness: serving others. In loving service to His disciples and to all people, Jesus showed His greatness. He humbled Himself to the point of giving up His life to save us from our sins.

A dispute also arose among them, as to which of them was to be regarded as the greatest. And [Jesus] said to them, ". . . Let the greatest among you become as the youngest, and the leader as one who serves. For who is the greater, one who reclines at table or one who serves? Is it not the one who reclines at table? But I am among you as the one who serves."

Luke 22:24-25, 26-27

Journal:

What would you like to be great at? How could you use that talent to serve others?

Pray:

Lord, forgive our pride, and lead us to serve You and others as You've served us. Amen.

J. S.

In the beginning was the Word, and the Word was with God, and the Word was God. . . . All things were made through Him, and without Him was not any thing made that was made. In Him was life, and the life was the light of men. The light shines in the darkness, and the darkness has not overcome it. . . . And the Word became flesh and dwelt among us, and we have seen His glory, glory as of the only Son from the Father, full of grace and truth.

John 1:1, 3–5, 14

And

People who use the word *and* a lot are usually excited. They have so much to tell that they can't wait for their next turn to speak. Or even their next sentence. They want to say what they want to say right now! And it's amazing!

Today's Scripture reading is packed full of "ands." The writer, John, had tons to say, and every word of it mattered. He wasn't just making a single point. He was sharing a history of creation and of salvation. Most of all, he was sharing the story of Jesus Christ, the Word made flesh.

John wanted us to know that Jesus isn't just one thing. He's not just a man. He's not just God. He's not just the light of the world. He's not just our source of life. He's not just our glorious Creator. He's all of these things, and so much more!

Most English teachers will tell you not start sentences with *and*, but the Book of John ignores that rule. And for good reason. John wanted to shout the exciting news that our Savior is God and made all things and is life and is light in the darkness and became a human baby and lived on earth and showed us His glory.

And His love for you goes on and on and on and on and . . .

Journal:

List things God does for you. And add more. And more.

Pray:

Lord, thank You that Your mercy has room for each and every one of us. Amen.   J. S.

You Are

For centuries, people have questioned whether God is a loving God. They look at the messy, messed-up world we live in and see its ugliness. They see this and wonder how a loving God could let it be such a mess. But the truth is that He's not the one who messed it up. God created a perfect world. Our sin broke it.

If you want proof of God's love for you, here it is: you are. You exist!

The very fact that there is a you, that you were born, shows God's love for you. God could have stayed in eternity by Himself or with the angels if He chose to make them. Instead, God made the world. He made flowers and trees and hedgehogs and dolphins and all the rest. And to crown His creation, He made people. He made us.

Don't stop there though. Through generations of people, God made your ancestors. Eventually, through your parents, He made you. He didn't have to do this. No one forced Him to do it. But He did it anyway because He wanted one more child to love and care for. He made you so that you could hear His Word and receive His gifts. He made you so that you could sing His praise and live in His kingdom.

Here's ultimate proof of a loving God: He sent His Son to die to redeem our messed-up world. He did it to save us.

Sing, O heavens, for the LORD has done it; shout, O depths of the earth; break forth into singing, O mountains, O forest, and every tree in it! For the LORD has redeemed Jacob, and will be glorified in Israel. Thus says the LORD, your Redeemer, who formed you from the womb: "I am the LORD, who made all things, who alone stretched out the heavens, who spread out the earth by Myself."

Isaiah 44:23–24

Journal:

How is every life a blessing?

Pray:

Father, help me to never forget Your love and to always share it with others. Amen.

J. S.

Consequently, when Christ came into the world, He said, "Sacrifices and offerings You have not desired, but a body have You prepared for Me; in burnt offerings and sin offerings You have taken no pleasure. Then I said, 'Behold, I have come to do Your will, O God, as it is written of Me in the scroll of the book.'"

Hebrews 10:5–7

Not It

"I have to finish cleaning Grandma's house today, and I can't do it alone. One of you is going to help me," said Mom.

"Help how?" Jace asked.

"Dust, vacuum, wash the windows, clean the toilets. It should only take a few hours."

"Not it!" Michael, Carson, and Braydon called instantly.

"Come on, guys," whined Jace. "It's always me."

That's what everyone shouts when a game of tag starts. "Not it!" Whoever's the slowest is stuck being "it" first. Jace's response makes sense too. No one wants to be the only one working when everyone else is having fun.

God the Father needed someone to suffer and die for the sins of the world. He knew who to ask—His Son, Jesus. This was an awful job, full of pain, suffering, and humiliation. Unlike when our parents "ask" us to do something, Jesus could have said no. He could have said, "No, I like heavenly glory a lot better." He could have said, "Fine, but I want a palace and rich parents." Or even, "I'll teach and heal, but the dying part is too much. Figure something else out, Father."

But Jesus didn't shout, "Not it!" and run away from death on the cross. Instead, He told His Father, "I have come to do Your will." And He did just that, suffering and dying to forgive your sins and mine.

Journal:

How can you help a parent, teacher, or friend by saying yes to something you don't want to do?

Pray:

Dear Jesus, thank You for choosing to do what Your Father asked. In Your name I pray. Amen.   J. S.

You Are a Child of the King

Picture a king in your mind. Did you picture a crown? beautiful clothes? a man sitting in a big throne? Those are all things that describe an earthly king in our world.

Our God is also our King! Our heavenly King is different from the kings we have on earth. God is the King of heaven and earth. In the Bible it tells us that we are children of God through our Baptism. I guess that means we are princes and princesses!

For in Christ Jesus you are all sons of God, through faith.

Galatians 3:26

As children of the heavenly King, we live our lives differently than other people who don't know about Jesus yet. Because Jesus loves us so much that He gave us His life to forgive our sins, we can share this Good News of His love to other people also! We get to tell other people about Jesus and pray for our friends. It is such a special feeling to be so loved by our Father in heaven!

Journal:

Draw a picture of yourself wearing a crown. Around your picture, make a list of people that you can tell about our King Jesus!

Pray:

Dear God, we are so thankful that You are our King and that we are Your sons and daughters. Help us have courage to tell others about You. We love You and want everyone to know about You. Amen.

L. K.

Give thanks to the
LORD, for He is good,
for His steadfast love
endures forever.

Psalm 136:1

He Is So Good

Think of a person you know who is a really good person. Are they always a good person? Even people who seem really super nice have bad days and make mistakes. We try our hardest to be kind to others at all times, but we are not always able to be kind. Because we have sin in our world, we are not able to be perfect on earth. No one can live perfectly on our earth except for Jesus.

When Jesus lived on earth, He lived a perfect life. He was kind to all people, all the time. We are so thankful to Jesus that He is so good. He lived as a perfect example for us to follow, and He loves us even when we are not following His ways perfectly. Jesus' love for us will go on forever!

This is really hard to understand . . . because we do not always deserve to be loved. Even when we are not kind to our friends, Jesus loves us! Even when we are not following the example given to us by Jesus, He still loves us! God loves us so much that He sent down His Son, Jesus, to die on a cross to pay for all of our sins. Many, many years before you were born, Jesus died on the cross and rose again from the dead. Even then, He was thinking of you because He loves you so much!

Journal:

Make a list of the things God does for you. Thank God for loving you even when you are sinful.

Pray:

Dear Jesus, thank You for being such a good God. Thank You for loving us even when we do not deserve to be loved. Amen.   *L. K.*

Is That What That's For?

Is it possible to put a pencil into your ear? Yes! Is it possible to cut your hair with a fingernail clipper? Sure! While these things are possible, why don't we do them? It's just a bad idea and could be harmful to you. In this same way, is it possible to break all of God's commandments? Unfortunately, yes!

While we are growing up, adults in our lives help us to use things the way they are intended to be used. We write with pencils and we cut our fingernails with the clippers. God never intended for us to be sinful people. Now, because we are sinful, He gives us the Ten Commandments, and rules to follow.

God promises to forgive us when we sin—so, does that mean that it is okay for us to just keep sinning? No! God didn't intend for us to live this way. He gives us these rules and guidelines for life in order to keep us safe. Just like adults do not want us to stick pencils into our ears or cut our hair with a fingernail clipper, God our Father keeps us safe by giving us guidelines for everyday living and His grace and love for when we are overtaken by sin and need forgiveness.

What shall we say then? Are we to continue in sin that grace may abound? By no means! How can we who died to sin still live in it? Do you not know that all of us who have been baptized into Christ Jesus were baptized into His death? We were buried therefore with Him by Baptism into death, in order that, just as Christ was raised from the dead by the glory of the Father, we too might walk in newness of life.

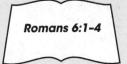

Romans 6:1–4

Journal:

Write about a time when you needed God's forgiveness. How do you know that He still loves you and forgives you every day?

Pray:

Dear Jesus, thank You for loving us and forgiving us even when we are sinful people. Thank You for keeping us safe and having plans for our lives. Continue to keep us safe and show us Your plans for our lives. Amen.   L. K.

Jesus Christ is the same yesterday and today and forever.

Hebrews 13:8

Forever

In the Old Testament, we read about the time before Jesus came to earth as a human. God the Father was known, and people were talking about Jesus and knew He would come, but He hadn't come yet. Today we know that Jesus is real! Jesus came and lived a perfect life on earth. He is the same Jesus that they talked about in the Old Testament.

Everything in our world is changing all the time. The weather changes. The sports teams change. The way you look changes as you grow. Everything changes.

But we can trust one thing for sure! Jesus Christ will never change! We know that He is always the same! What we read about Jesus in the Old Testament is still true today and will be true forever! Forever is a really long time . . . our human brains cannot even begin to understand how long forever is. Jesus will never change the way that He forgives, loves, listens, or lives forever.

Journal:

Draw a picture of Jesus. Around your picture, add details about Jesus.

Pray:

Dear Jesus, it is so amazing that You never change! We thank You that Your love for us will always be the same and that we can trust You forever and ever. Thank You for being our great and mighty God. Amen. L. K.

Where Did You Come From?

Do you know anyone who has had a baby? Maybe your mom or an aunt or a lady from your church? Do you ever wonder how the baby grows inside of them? It is totally a miracle! The baby starts from a tiny, tiny cell and grows and grows until it is big and strong enough to live outside of its mother's body.

This is how you grew also. Do you think the mother has to think every day about how she will grow that baby? Does she have to do the work herself? No, it all just happens inside of her body.

In Jeremiah, we are told that God knew who we were before we were formed inside of our mother. God does the work of creating every baby into exactly who He intended the baby to be. It also says that before we were born God set us apart. He chooses us as His people and marks us as His own in our Baptism. We are all very special in our own way. Yet, we are all loved by God more than we can ever understand—so much so that He sent Jesus to be our Savior from sin.

> Before I formed you in the womb I knew you, and before you were born I consecrated you; I appointed you a prophet to the nations.
>
> *Jeremiah 1:5*

Journal:

Write a thank-you note to God for how He created you. Write about the things that make you happy, the things you like doing, and the people you like being around.

Pray:

Dear Jesus, You are such an amazing God. Thank You for knowing me even before I was born. Thank You for making everyone a little bit different and for loving us all the same. Amen. L. K.

So, whether you eat or drink, or whatever you do, do all to the glory of God.

1 Corinthians 10:31

For the Glory of God

Every day of our lives, we do so many things. Eating, playing, cleaning, talking, resting, helping . . . the list goes on. Some of those things are very fun! We thank God every day that He allows us to live a life full of such wonderful things! But what about our chores? Do we thank God for the chores that we have to do?

Maybe not . . . but we should! We should find a way to praise God in everything we do! If you do not love to take out the trash at your house but it is your chore, maybe you could praise God for your family who created all of this trash together. If you do not love helping with yard work, you could praise God for the beauty of the creation of your yard. In every task, there is a reason to praise God and give Him the glory. Thank God that your body is able to help your friends and family. Thank Him that you have food to eat while you help clear the table after dinner.

God is so good! We can give Him glory at all times. He gave us everything through His Son, Jesus, who died and rose again to save us from our sins.

Journal:

Draw a line down the middle of your paper. On one side, make a list of the chores or activities that are not your favorite. On the other side, write a reason to praise God while you do that chore or activity.

Pray:

Dear Jesus, You give us so much in life. Today we thank You that we are able to be helpful to the people around us. Help us to remember how good You are to us while we go through our days. We love and praise Your name! Amen.   L. K.

Rejoice

Life is not always full of happy things. Because there is sin in the world, we also have really sad things in our world—like death, fighting, and sickness. During those times, it is really hard to remember that we have a God who is really good.

In Philippians, we are reminded to rejoice in the Lord always! We can always find a reason to rejoice in the Lord. Even during a sad time in our life, we can rejoice in the Lord that we are still breathing or that there is food on our table for meals. The Bible does not tell us that life will always be good, but it does tell us that our God will always be good! We get to live in the promise that our God is a loving God who is always with us. We are never alone. We can rejoice in that promise!

Rejoice in the Lord always; again I will say, rejoice.

Philippians 4:4

Journal:

Draw a big smiley face on your paper. In and around the smiley face, draw and write reasons that you can rejoice. They can be big reasons and little reasons. We can rejoice in the Lord always!

Pray:

Dear Jesus, we thank You today that You are a good God! Thank You for giving us reasons to rejoice even when our world is full of sadness and sin. Thank You for giving us people in our lives whom we love and can rejoice with. We love You. Amen.   L. K.

July

Bible puzzles, games, and activities

Solutions on page 80

Places I Go

Write a way you can praise and thank God wherever you go.

Be What You Already Are!

Read the situation in the middle column. What would you do? Draw an arrow to the "saintly" answer, and put an X over the "sinner" answer.

I would . . .	Saint or Sinner?	I would . . .
Look the other way and pretend I saw nothing.	I see a classmate getting picked on at recess.	Go over, tell the bully to go away, and invite the classmate to play with me.
Help pick them up.	Somebody drops their books and papers all over the hallway.	Point and laugh with my friends.
Tell my friend I'll be over as soon as I can finish my homework.	I have lots of homework to do, and my friend invites me over to play.	Tell my parents I'm finished with all my homework even when I'm not, so they'll let me go.
Pretend I didn't notice.	The new kid at school forgot to bring a lunch.	Share mine.
Say, "Only if you're sure we won't get caught."	My best friend asks to copy off my test paper.	Say, "I can't do that, but we could study together."

My Coloring Page

July Journal

Puzzle 1 Answer

Be What You Already Are!

Read the situation in the middle column. What would you do? Draw an arrow to the "saintly" answer, and put an X over the "sinner" answer.

I would . . .	Saint or Sinner?	I would . . .
Look the other way and pretend I saw nothing.	I see a classmate getting picked on at recess.	Go over, tell the bully to go away, and invite the classmate to play with me.
Help pick them up.	Somebody drops their books and papers all over the hallway.	Point and laugh with my friends.
Tell my friend I'll be over as soon as I can finish my homework.	I have lots of homework to do, and my friend invites me over to play.	Tell my parents I'm finished with all my homework even when I'm not, so they'll let me go.
Pretend I didn't notice.	The new kid at school forgot to bring a lunch.	Share mine.
Say, "Only if you're sure we won't get caught."	My best friend asks to copy off my test paper.	Say, "I can't do that, but we could study together."

AUGUST

June–August 2019
Vol. 61, Issue No. 4

Daily Readings for Young Christians

Contributors to the August devotions:

Rebekah Curtis, Gretchen Gebhardt, Dennis Goff,
Morgan Grillott, Carrie Kober, Christine Weerts

Edited by Mark S. Sengele

Then desire when it has conceived gives birth to sin, and sin when it is fully grown brings forth death.

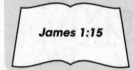

James 1:15

Splinters and Sinners

Elaina and Alex loved their new play set. It had a huge twisty slide, a rock climbing wall, an intricate rope ladder leading to a lookout tower, two big swings, and much, much more. The only problem was if they were not careful, they might get a splinter or two while playing on the wooden structure.

One day, Elaina got a small splinter in her thumb. She tried hiding it from her mom and dad. She didn't like having splinters taken out. But over the next few days, her thumb became tender and uncomfortable. Soon, it hurt all the time! One evening, her mother reached out to grasp her hand, and Elaina cried out in pain. Her mom discovered the splinter!

Elaina's father worked to remove the splinter. Even though he was careful, it was still painful. Afterward, her parents explained that, if they had removed the splinter right away, the experience would not have caused her so much pain. Instead, by keeping the splinter in, the skin around became infected.

Elaina's splinter problem is much like our sin. When we hide or ignore our sins, they don't go away. They only get worse and end up hurting us even more. We need Jesus to remove our sins.

To get rid of them, God leads us to repent, to feel sorry for them. Then we confess our sins to God. He promises to forgive our sins for Jesus' sake. He wipes them away. God accepts our repentant hearts and forgives our sins. Through Jesus, we are made new; our sins are forgiven.

So, don't be afraid! Let Jesus take out that splinter of sin!

Journal:

If you are hiding a sin, consider repenting. In your journal, write "Jesus, Savior, have mercy on me."

Pray:

Dear Jesus, please forgive me for trying to hide my sins from You. Help me repent of my sins and bring them to You. Thank You for forgiving me and renewing me. Amen.

C. K.

True or False?

There are many different teachings and beliefs about God. Some are true, but many are false. Often, false teachings confuse us because they sound close to the truth. You must be careful when hearing some beliefs. For example, are these statements true or false?

1. Jesus is both true man and true God.
2. Only good people go to heaven.
3. All religions are basically similar; any one will get you to heaven.
4. Faith is a gift from God.
5. The Bible is not true.

How do you keep false teachings from leading you astray? First, ask yourself if the teachings point to Jesus as our Savior. Then test the teachings against God's Word. How can you do this? Continue to read, learn, and study God's Word. You can regularly attend church and Sunday School. Ask your pastor, teacher, and parents to help answer more difficult questions.

Consider these responses to the statements above.

1. True. Jesus became true man to take our place; He is true God to save us from our sins (Matthew 8:20; 1 John 5:20).
2. False. All people are sinners. We get to heaven only through the saving blood of Jesus (Romans 3:23–24).
3. False. The only true religion is Christianity, where the name of Jesus is taught and confessed (1 John 5:12; 1 Timothy 2:5).
4. True. We cannot by our own power believe in Jesus. Faith and salvation are gifts from God (Ephesians 2:8–9).
5. False. The Bible is the true Word of God, written by man, but inspired by the Holy Spirit. It teaches us to trust in Jesus for forgiveness (2 Timothy 3:16).

So that we may no longer be children, tossed to and fro by the waves and carried about by every wind of doctrine, by human cunning, by craftiness in deceitful schemes. Rather, speaking the truth in love, we are to grow up in every way into Him who is the head, into Christ.

Ephesians 4:14–15

Journal:

What is a question you have about your faith? Write it in your journal.

Pray:

Dear God, help me know Your truth. Guide me through Your Word to know You better. In Jesus' name I pray. Amen.

C. K.

The Sun, the Light

There was a man sent from God, whose name was John. He came as a witness, to bear witness about the light, that all might believe through him. He was not the light, but came to bear witness about the light. The true light, which gives light to everyone, was coming into the world.

John 1:6–9

On a hot summer day, it's great to take a dip in the cool water of a pool or a lake. Then, you can set out your favorite beach towel, lie down, and enjoy the warmth of the sun's rays. In the fall, when you feel the chill of a crisp wind, you can search for a spot in the sun and let it warm your body. In the winter when the days are short and dreary, you welcome a sunny day like you would a long-lost friend coming to visit. Then comes spring. It ushers in longer daylight hours. You see plants begin to grow. All year long, the sun brings light, warmth, and even joy.

Long ago, John came into the world to bear witness to a different light. That light was Jesus Christ. He is the true light, the one who came to cast out the darkness of sin. He did that by dying on the cross on a dark Friday we now call Good. He rose early in the morning on Easter to prove His victory over death. He ascended into heaven and sits at the right hand of God. Yet mysteriously, He is also with His children, shining through His Word and Sacraments. Those who believe in Jesus as their Savior have the light of salvation.

In heaven, there will be no need for the sun, but there will be light. The Bible tells us that God will be the light of heaven. His presence will bring much more light, warmth, and happiness than the sun. In fact, it will be perfect.

Journal:

Compare the light of the sun with Jesus, the light of your salvation.

Pray:

Dear Jesus, in You there is no darkness of sin. You are all light—the light of my salvation. But I daily sin and need Your forgiveness. Please grant it to me now, and keep me as Your child forever. Amen.
C. K.

Don't Get Lost!

The Drew family was on an unfamiliar road, heading home from an exciting trip to the Black Hills. It was late, and they were eager to plop down in their own beds. Dad said, "I wonder if that other road would take us back to the main highway."

Mom was dozing off, but Jared offered his dad a little advice. "Dad, remember what happened the last time we didn't follow the GPS? Maybe we should just follow the plan."

"I suppose you're right," Dad agreed. "We don't want to get lost again! Even though this road feels unfamiliar, I suppose we should simply trust the GPS. Good thinking, Jared."

After a surprising left turn and miles of orange cones around construction, the old familiar roads came into view. And sure enough, just before midnight, the Drew family arrived home safely.

You make known to me the path of life; in Your presence there is fullness of joy; at Your right hand are pleasures forevermore.

Psalm 16:11

The GPS kept the Drew family going the right way. Who guides God's children through life? God does, of course. He is the path of life. With Him, we have joy. With Him, have the sure and certain hope of heaven.

Often, our sin and pride tempt us to take another road to heaven. We want to be in charge. We think we know a better way. The devil, too, tries to lead us down the wrong roads. His temptations can be quite appealing.

What a blessing it is to have God's Word. Through it, we hear that God is active in our lives. He saved us through Jesus. He forgives our sins and guides us through troubles. He has prepared a homecoming for us in heaven.

Yes, praise be to God, who makes known to us the path of life now and forever.

Journal:

Describe a time when you decided not to follow God's Word. How did you get back on the right path?

Pray:

Dear God, thank You for Your Word and for making known to me the path of life, now and forever. In Jesus' name I pray. Amen.   C. K.

If we say we have no sin, we deceive ourselves, and the truth is not in us. If we confess our sins, He is faithful and just to forgive us our sins and to cleanse us from all unrighteousness. If we say we have not sinned, we make Him a liar, and His word is not in us.

1 John 1:8–10

Overdoing It

Grab a piece of paper and try this. Make a list of all the sports teams you play on in a year. Add to that list the clubs or groups in which you participate. Then add the kinds of lessons you take. Then finish the list by including any special projects or chores you do.

Whew! What a list! Do you ever feel overwhelmed with your schedule or your to-do list? Are there days when you don't know if you can get it all done? Are you ever so busy that you simply can't find time to relax?

When God, who commands that He be first in our lives, is not even on the list, we are overdoing it big time. When He is forgotten, our lives are out of order and topsy-turvy. When we are too tired to pray, too busy for church and Sunday School, or too willing to ignore reading our Bibles, we are too, too distracted. When we're that busy, we miss out on the nourishment of God's Word, the chance to focus on the needs of others, the support of our church family, and the time to talk to our heavenly Father in prayer.

How do we overcome overdoing it? We do it through the power of God, and confession is a good way to start. We can ask God to forgive us for not placing Him as the most important thing in our lives. Since God is faithful and just, He will forgive our sins. He will cleanse us from all unrighteousness.

Through His Word and Sacraments, God strengthens our faith. Through the power of our Baptisms, He renews us daily, so the "new man" in us can rise up and make new lists that include Him and service to others in His name.

Journal:

As a family, talk about how you use God's gift of time. What ways can your family make God number one?

Pray:

Lord, forgive me when I put other things ahead of You. Help me slow down and make more time to pray and to study Your Word. Amen. C. K.

Slow Down!

At baseball practice, Luke and his teammates were arguing. Each player claimed to be the fastest runner on the team. To settle the argument, they decided to have a race. As the race began, Luke tripped over his shoelace and fell. Of course, Luke finished last! For the rest of the evening, he was in a grumpy mood. Luke felt horrible. Now he was known as the slowest runner on the team.

Have you ever wanted to be the best, the fastest, or the first at something? God tells us being "fast" is not always the best thing for us. In fact, in our Bible reading, God tells us to be slow!

God's Word tells us to be slow to speak. What does this mean? It means to think about what we are going to say before saying it. Sometimes, we make fun of others or foolishly blurt out hurtful, critical, or unkind words. Angry words fly out of our mouths before we think about what we are saying! If you're guilty of this, you are not alone.

Know this, my beloved brothers: let every person be quick to hear, slow to speak, slow to anger; for the anger of man does not produce the righteousness of God.

James 1:19–20

God also tells us to be slow to anger. It is easy to get caught up in our emotions and let our tempers get the best of us. We think, I have a right to be angry! But God tells us to put a halt on our anger and stop it in its tracks before we go any further. If you are guilty of this, you are not alone.

Fast or slow, we are people who need time to say we're sorry and to hear His words of forgiveness. We need time to thank Jesus for being our Savior. We need time to ask for His help.

So, as you speed up to listen or slow down to speak, remember the good and perfect gifts that come to you from God.

Journal:

The Bible reading says we should "be quick to hear" (v. 19). Write what you think that means.

Pray:

Dear Jesus, help me to slow down and think about the things that I say and do; let them reflect to others my love for You. Amen.   *C. K.*

Even the darkness is not dark to You; the night is bright as the day, for darkness is as light with You.

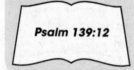

Psalm 139:12

X-ray Eyes

During the day, Emily appreciated the big oak tree outside her bedroom window. She spent hours climbing its branches, getting a bird's-eye view of the neighborhood. On hot days, she'd lie under its shade and watch the clouds sail by.

At night, that tree turned into a monster. Its large branches made shadows against her window. In the slightest wind, the tree creaked and moaned. In a storm, the branches scratched against her window. At those times, she grabbed the covers and pulled them over her head.

Emily's father tried to comfort her and explain it was the same tree she climbed during the day, but his words didn't help. He put a night-light in the hall, but its tiny glow was no match for Emily's fear.

One night when her cousin Lydia was staying with her, the wind began howling. The tree monster came to life. Emily grabbed for her cousin. Lydia wanted to help, so she said, "I used to be scared of our neighbor's dog at night. It howled and barked. I would run to my mom's room and jump into her bed. So my mom had me memorize a psalm to help me. Wanna hear it?"

Lydia continued as the wind howled. "'Even the darkness is not dark to You; the night is bright as the day, for darkness is as light with You.' Just think, Em—there's no darkness to God. He sees everything, all the time."

Emily smiled. "It's like God has x-ray eyes," she said.

God is powerful. He sees all things. God is omniscient. He knows all things. God is forgiving. When the devil uses our sins to scare us into thinking that God could not love us, God forgives us for Jesus' sake. Nothing can take us away from God's love in Christ. It guards our faith, forgives our sins, and gives us eternal life.

Journal:

What scares people your age? Make a list.

Pray:

Dear God, thank You for Your x-ray eyes, which watch over me day and night. Keep me from fears that make me doubt Your love. Amen.   C. W.

Ice-Cream Sunday

Dad called upstairs to the boys, "Hunter and Jesse, don't forget your sunglasses."

"Sunglasses?" Jesse asked.

"Remember, church is outside this morning," Dad reminded him.

"Why is church outside?" Hunter asked.

Dad didn't really know how to answer that question. He didn't know why Pastor Dan decided to have an outdoor service today.

On the way home, Dad asked the boys what they thought of having church outside. "I liked it," they both said. "Especially the ice cream after church."

"I agree, but do you remember why we were outside?" Dad asked.

"Yeah," Jesse said. "Pastor said to look at the cars zooming by and think about the people in them."

Then He said to His disciples, "The harvest is plentiful, but the laborers are few."

Matthew 9:37

"You're right, Jesse," Dad responded. "Pastor preached about how the 'harvest is plentiful.' When we think of a harvest out in the country, we usually think of the bushels of corn, wheat, or beans the farmers pick each year. But when Jesus said, 'The harvest is plentiful,' He was talking about His kingdom, about nurturing the seed of faith God plants in His people. Maybe some people who drove by this morning don't know Jesus. Having church outside reminds us how Jesus died to forgive their sins too. So what do you think about doing this kind of service again, boys?"

Jesse said it was a good reminder to pray for and serve others. Hunter laughed and said, "Sure, especially if we have another harvest of ice cream!"

Journal:

Write the names of two people you know who don't believe in Jesus.

Pray:

Dear God, please bring _____ to know You and believe in You. Help me to share Jesus with people who don't yet know You. Amen.   D. G.

I tell you, there is joy before the angels of God over one sinner who repents.

Luke 15:10

What Was Lost Is Found

Carlos had mountains of cardboard boxes in his bedroom. He was digging in them without success to find one particular item. Finally, he called out, "Mom, have you seen my glove? I've looked everywhere."

Carlos and his mother had just moved into a new house. Things were still in chaos. There were dishes in the living room and books in the bathroom. But Carlos was eager to find that glove. He wanted to make some new friends, and the neighborhood boys had invited him to play ball.

Soon, he heard his mom call out, "Carlos, I found it!" Carlos came running. He gave his mom a hug and ran off to the corner lot. "I hope you make some new friends," said Mom.

After supper, during family devotions, Carlos's mother read Jesus' parable of the lost coin. "Carlos," said Mom, "the woman in the parable searched her whole house to find the lost coin. That reminds me of searching everywhere for your baseball glove today. I think we were both excited to find the glove. But that search is not as important as God's search for sinners who are lost in darkness. We need Jesus to seek us. We need Him to hear our confession and forgive our sins."

"I know what happens next. There is great rejoicing. Right?"

"Yes, Carlos," Mom continued, "that's right. The Bible says the angels rejoice when one sinner repents."

"Then I have an idea," Carlos said with a glint in his eye.

"What is it?" Mom asked.

"Why don't we rejoice with root-beer floats?"

Mom agreed and said, "Right after you say the prayer, I'll search for the ice-cream scoop!"

Journal:

Write a description of how valuable God thinks you are.

Pray:

Dear God, thank You for searching for me and finding me. Thank You for coming to me in Baptism and making me Your child forever and ever. In Jesus' name I pray. Amen.

D. G.

That Was Heavy!

Lauren asked her dad for help. The box was too heavy for her to get up to her room.

"Ugh!" said her dad. "This box is so heavy! What do you have in here, Lauren? A bunch of rocks?"

"Well, actually, yes," Lauren admitted.

Lauren was collecting rocks. Her science teacher got her interested in their sizes, shapes, and colors. So she started her own collection, but she didn't realize how heavy they were until she started carrying them upstairs.

[Cast] all your anxieties on Him, because He cares for you.

1 Peter 5:7

"I'm sorry the box was so heavy, Dad. Collecting rocks is part of my plan to do better in science this year."

Dad smiled. "Then I'm sure you will learn a lot of valuable information and be able to share what you know. When you are ready to take your collection to school one day, I'll be glad to carry it for you."

Heavy loads are easy for some people to carry and harder for others. A box of rocks and a week of tests are both heavy burdens, but they are different too. The worries, fears, or problems in life can weigh us down. Like Lauren's box of rocks, they are too much for us. We need help. The apostle Peter wrote some good news about God. He said we can cast our anxieties on God because "He cares for you" (1 Peter 5:7).

God sent Jesus to take care of our biggest problem—our sin. When He died on the cross, Jesus carried the weight of our sins and the sins of the whole world. He died that we might be forgiven. If He can do that, He can certainly carry the weight of whatever worries you and I have.

Journal:

What worries or problems weigh you down? Write a prayer about them.

Pray:

Dear Jesus, thank You for carrying the worries and the fears that I have in life and for carrying all my sins to the cross. Amen.   *D. G.*

Rejoice in the Lord always; again I will say, rejoice.

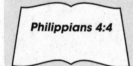

Philippians 4:4

Happy or Joyful

David, who was usually riding his bike, wasn't. He sat on the porch swing, swaying back and forth. His dad was curious about this quiet behavior and joined him. "What's up, David?"

"I'm really sad that Brian has to be in the hospital."

"Me too," said Dad. "But Brian's cancer is serious."

David looked up with questioning eyes. "Then how can Brian have such a strong faith when he is so sick?"

"I noticed Brian's faith too," said Dad. "I think Brian has real joy."

"Yeah, Brian is a funny guy. He always makes me laugh."

"That's true, David," said his dad, "but I'm talking about a different kind of joy. It's the joy we read about in Philippians, where the apostle Paul says, 'Rejoice in the Lord always; again I will say, rejoice.' That kind of joy is not the same thing as being happy. When the apostle Paul wrote those words, he was in prison for telling others about Jesus. He wasn't happy about being in prison, but he still had joy."

Then David asked, "So the kind of joy Paul talks about is different from telling jokes and being funny?"

Dad continued, "I think so. Paul's sense of joy, and the kind of joy I see in Brian, comes from belonging to Jesus, from being His child. Brian believes Jesus gives him strength to go through every treatment and surgery. Brian also knows his church family is praying for him, and that's a comfort. Even if he isn't cured, Brian knows someday he will be in heaven with Jesus."

"I'm glad Brian has that kind of joy now, Dad. But I will be so happy when he gets out of the hospital."

"Me too, David."

Journal:

Write about the difference between happiness and rejoicing in the Lord.

Pray:

Dear God, help me rejoice at all times, knowing I am Yours and You are mine. In Jesus' name I pray. Amen.

D. G.

At Home with God

Amanda hopped up the steps into Sarah's cabin and walked into her room. "Oh dear!" she said. Amanda could tell Sarah was homesick. "Would you like to walk with me to the camp counselors' office? I happen to know the kitchen staff brings fresh cookies for the camp counselors about this time of day. If you like, you could call your mom and dad."

Sarah smiled and went with Amanda. She talked with her parents on the phone. It helped. Then the girls munched on fresh chocolate-chip cookies and walked past the lake to join the campers.

"Sarah, you are not the first camper to get homesick. The first time I came to camp here when I was your age, I was really lonely."

"Really?" Sarah was surprised.

"Absolutely. It is common to feel homesick. Even in Bible times, it happened. Think about the story of Ruth in the Old Testament. Ruth's mother-in-law, Naomi, had lost her husband and their two sons. So Naomi went back to the country where she used to live. She heard there was food there. Maybe she was homesick too. Her daughter-in-law Ruth insisted on going with her. Through those lonely times, God continued His plan of salvation."

But Ruth said, "Do not urge me to leave you or to return from following you. For where you go I will go, and where you lodge I will lodge. Your people shall be my people, and your God my God."

Ruth 1:16

"I remember that story," said Sarah. "Eventually, God gave Ruth a husband, and their child became the grandfather of King David. It was all part of God's plan, all right."

"Even when you feel alone, Sarah, God is at work. Through Baptism, God brought you into His family and you received Jesus' gifts—forgiveness, life, and salvation. You, too, are part of His great salvation story. Even when you are away from home, you can be at-home with God."

Journal:

Write about a time when you felt homesick. What reminds you of God's love for you when you are away from home?

Pray:

Dear God, help me feel at home with You when I am away from my family and friends. Amen.   D. G.

13

• • • • • • • • • •
Tuesday
• • • • • • • • • •

I know how to be brought low, and I know how to abound. In any and every circumstance, I have learned the secret of facing plenty and hunger, abundance and need. I can do all things through Him who strengthens me.

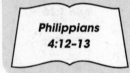

Philippians 4:12–13

Which Tent Do You Live In?

"Tommy," called Dad, "let's get a new tent for our camping trip."

At the store, Tommy picked out the biggest tent he could find. "How about this one, Dad?"

"Tommy, that tent is way too big. We don't need such a large tent for just the two of us. And remember, we are hiking to our campsite. I don't want to hike with a big tent like this on my back. How about this one instead?" Tommy's dad pointed to another tent. "I think this one will be comfortable for the two of us."

On their way home, Tommy's dad remembered something the other fathers had talked about at their men's Bible study that morning. "Tommy, the apostle Paul says in Philippians, 'I have learned in whatever situation I am to be content' (4:11). Which tent did Paul live in, Tommy?"

"What do you mean, Dad?"

"Well, Paul said he learned the secret of how to be content in any situation. So, which tent did he live in? Content or discontent?"

"Huh?"

"Tommy, a lot of times we find ourselves feeling discontent because we don't have everything we want in life. But we can learn to be content with the blessings God gives us. After all, God gives us what we need most in life—His forgiveness through Jesus Christ. God gives us His love, and He promises to be with us always. God gives us the promise of heaven. Knowing and believing in God's good gifts can lead us to be content in life, whatever the situation."

"Hey, Dad, can I make a sign for our tent that says 'Content'?"

"That's a great idea, Tommy."

Journal:

What are some times in life when you feel content? What are some times when you feel discontent? How can your discontentment turn into contentment?

Pray:

Dear God, help me be content in Jesus with the blessings You give me in life. Amen.   *D. G.*

From Hot to Cold

"Everyone, get your swimsuits and towels. We're going to the lake for the day. It's way too hot to stay home," Mrs. O'Rourke announced after breakfast one morning. "The lake stays cool even during this heat. It will feel refreshing to spend the day in the water."

After a picnic lunch at the lake and an afternoon of swimming, the O'Rourke family headed back home. On the way, Mr. O'Rourke noticed that the temperature gauge in the car read 100 degrees. "Wow! It was really hot today," he said. "And just think," he said, "six months from now the temperature could be 100 degrees less than it is today. What a huge difference a few months makes!"

Later, during family devotions, Mr. O'Rourke read from Psalm 103. He was still thinking of the dramatic difference between the heat of summer and the bitter cold of winter. In this psalm, David recognized a huge difference when he said, "As far as the east is from the west, so far does He remove our transgressions from us" (v. 12). When David talks about how far God removes our sins, it's kind of like comparing the dramatic difference between February's zero temperatures and August's 100 degrees.

But the steadfast love of the LORD is from everlasting to everlasting on those who fear Him, and His righteousness to children's children, to those who keep His covenant and remember to do His commandments.

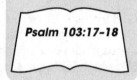

Psalm 103:17–18

The difference between those two extremes is nothing compared to what God does through the power of Jesus Christ's death and resurrection. God separates our sins from our lives. We may remember the wrongs we have done, but God doesn't. We may not forget the mistakes we have made, but God does. Through Jesus Christ, God removes our sins from us as far as the east is from the west. Yes, God has dramatic love for us!

Journal:

Write down the names of two cities that are far apart. God removes your sins ever farther than the distance between those two cities.

Pray:

Dear God, thank You for removing my sins from me and for not remembering them anymore. Help me forgive others too. In Jesus' name I pray. Amen.   D. G.

Bless the LORD, O my soul, and all that is within me, bless His holy name!

Psalm 103:1

Thy Name

"What's new?" Mom asked.

"Mrs. Lerner showed us the plaque she got from the church for being a teacher at our school for twenty-five years. It says, 'To God be the glory' on it. Why did they write that? She's the one who has been doing all the work," Ann said.

"Mrs. Lerner was a faithful teacher," Mom said, "but she couldn't have done it without God's help. He gave her the ability to teach. He gave her strength and willingness to do it. I'm glad they gave her a plaque. Did you ask her what she thought about the words?"

"She liked them," Ann answered. "She said she lives every day in God's grace—in His love. She wants to use her gifts to glorify God, and she doesn't want to teach or say anything about God that is false or misleading."

"What a good answer! As Christians, we are part of God's Body. The new and forgiven person wants to live the new life God has given us, but our sinfulness gets in the way. Sometimes, we give in to temptation. We sin. We do things God forbids us to do, and we may lead others away from God," Mom said.

"You mean like when we lie, curse, or swear?" Ann asked.

"That's right. That's why in the Lord's Prayer we pray, 'Hallowed be Thy name.' God's name is holy because He is holy. When we sin, we profane His name. We pray that God would help us live holy lives. When that happens, we keep God's name holy in our lives," Mom explained.

"Help me, Jesus, to praise and honor You in what I say and do," Ann prayed. "And thank You for Mom and Mrs. Lerner and for everyone who has helped me learn about You."

Journal:

What are some ways to honor God's name?

Pray:

Dear Jesus, in Baptism, You gave me Your name. Forgive me when I do not hallow it. Thank You for working in me, that I might glorify You in all I do and say. Help me to keep Your name holy. Amen.   G. G.

The Kingdom of God

"It's not fair," Greta wailed. "The boys say they are Kings of the Elm. If I want to play in the tree house, I have to be ten years old, five feet tall, and a boy!"

"Why don't you help me in the kitchen? You can be Queen of Cooking or Princess of the Pots," suggested Mom.

"But I want to be part of a special kingdom!" Greta insisted.

"Oh, you are, Greta," Mom said. "Do you remember the part of the Lord's Prayer that talks about God's kingdom?"

"'Thy kingdom come.' That's what I want!" exclaimed Greta.

"Well, you are part of the kingdom of God, Greta. When you were a baby, you were baptized in the name of the Father and of the Son and of the Holy Spirit. The pastor put water on you, and you were forever changed," Mom said.

Jesus answered, "Truly, truly, I say to you, unless one is born of water and the Spirit, he cannot enter the kingdom of God."

John 3:5

"How was I changed?" Greta asked.

"In Baptism, the Holy Spirit worked faith in your heart. You became a part of God's kingdom. Jesus referred to Baptism as being born again," Mom said. "You didn't look any different, but you became an heir of heaven."

"Are the boys part of this kingdom too?" Greta asked.

"Yes, the boys were baptized too, Greta. We love them too much to leave them out. Someday, Jesus will come again and will take all His children to live with Him forever. It will be a great day," Mom said. "It will be the end of disappointments and the beginning of joy."

Greta said. "I think we should talk about it at supper so the boys know what the kingdom of God is all about."

"That's a good idea!"

Journal:

God is an eternal, generous King. What gifts has He poured out on you?

Pray:

Dear Lord, may Your Word be preached properly, so the kingdom of God may come to those who are not yet in it. Thank You for the gifts You so graciously give me. In Jesus' name I pray. Amen.

G. G.

Our Father Knows Best

Years ago, there was a television show called *Father Knows Best*. The children in this TV family often got into trouble because they made poor decisions. Sometimes, their feelings were hurt; other times, they hurt someone else's feelings. However, when they went to talk to their dad about their problems, he lovingly helped them to see their mistakes. He helped them decide what they should do about it. The father always knew what was best for his children, even if it was not what they wanted.

How true this is about our heavenly Father also! When we sin, we can go to our Father, confess our sin, and receive His forgiveness. When we are hurt or in trouble, He comforts and guides us.

We do not always know what is best for us, so we ask our heavenly Father to do what He knows is best. Sometimes, this means giving up what we want so that we can receive something better.

We pray in the Lord's Prayer, "Thy will be done on earth as it is in heaven." God's will is always good and perfect. He knows that the devil is our enemy. He knows what we need to remain strong in faith and to avoid the things that will lead us away from Him.

In the Garden of Gethsemane, Jesus prayed, "Thy will be done." God's will was that Jesus would suffer for all of our sins, die, and be raised again. Because Jesus followed the will of the Father, our sins are forgiven, and we also will be raised from the dead. We can look forward to celebrating with Him in heaven, where there will be no more mistakes, no more hurt, and no more sadness.

Our Father always gives us His best!

For I have come down from heaven, not to do My own will but the will of Him who sent Me. And this is the will of Him who sent Me, that I should lose nothing of all that He has given Me, but raise it up on the last day.

John 6:38-39

Journal:

What problems do you need your heavenly Father to solve?

Pray:

Dear Father, thank You for giving me Your best, especially for sending Jesus to be my Savior. Please guide me through my troubles, and teach me to pray, "Thy will be done." Amen.

G. G.

"All things are lawful," but not all things are helpful. "All things are lawful," but not all things build up. Let no one seek his own good, but the good of his neighbor.

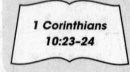

1 Corinthians 10:23–24

Socks and Sins

Is it a sin if you ask for something without saying please?

Is it a sin if you only eat cake for lunch?

Is it a sin if you don't change your socks for four days?

We all know that we're not supposed to sin. But you can probably think of some rules that don't make sense to you. Does that mean that you're free to ignore them?

Christians follow rules to keep the Fourth Commandment: Honor your father and your mother. Rules are made by people whom God has given authority over us. Obeying rules is how we honor God and those authorities.

We also follow rules—even rules that aren't exactly about sins—because rules protect people and help people get along. Saying please when you ask for something shows respect. Eating your sandwich and apple keeps you healthy. Wearing clean socks keeps the air smelling sweet for the other people breathing it.

Jesus showed His love for us by dying for our sins and sharing His resurrection with us. We show love for one another by dying to things we want and putting other people's needs and feelings first. Change those socks! Your friends won't arrest you if you don't, but they'll thank you if you do.

Journal:

What's a rule that isn't your favorite? Who are the people you serve when you keep it?

Pray:

Dear Jesus, everything You do is for my good. Help me to think about what's good for others and to serve them like You serve me. Amen.   R. C.

Division Problems

Have you ever been in a group of people who got along perfectly? No way! Everyone knows that when you get people together, there are going to be disagreements. You don't like my shirt, and I don't like how you eat Jell-O. Your dad doesn't want a dog. Your teacher plays awful music by Beethoven or Prince during lunch. Your friend badmouths you, and you badmouth her right back. No family, group of friends, classroom, or church can get away from disagreement. Sins make us disagree and act disagreeably.

What's the solution? Should we all find dark little caves where we can hide for the rest of our lives and not bother one another with our slurpy Jell-O eating and mean words? No! If we ran away from one another, we would be more divided than ever. The first step to fixing our divisions is to remember what we have in common. We are all sinners, and we all need a Savior. There is only one Jesus who died to forgive us and rose to give us life. When sinners cling to Him, we'll find ourselves clinging to one another too.

For, in the first place, when you come together as a church, I hear that there are divisions among you. And I believe it in part, for there must be factions among you in order that those who are genuine among you may be recognized.

1 Corinthians 11:18–19

Journal:

Tell about a time when you saw some divided people handle their differences well.

Pray:

Lord Jesus, forgive us our trespasses as we forgive those who trespass against us. Help us to live at peace with one another, since You made peace with us. Amen.   R. C.

Therefore I want you to understand that no one speaking in the Spirit of God ever says "Jesus is accursed!" and no one can say "Jesus is Lord" except in the Holy Spirit.

1 Corinthians 12:3

Who's Your Lord?

If Darth Vader were your boss, what would you call him? Darth? Anakin? Mr. Vader? No, you'd call him Lord Vader. We don't call people who outrank us by their first names. Miss, Mrs., or Mr. show personal respect. Titles like "Doctor," "Judge," or "Pastor" recognize a person's expertise and position. "Lord" is stronger. To call someone "Lord" means that he is the absolute boss. He is above you in everything, and you take orders from him.

Once, you were so lost in sin that Jesus was not the Lord you were looking for. Jesus became your Lord when the Holy Spirit gave you the gift of faith in Holy Baptism. Then you knew you were made to follow, trust, and obey a good God. There is no better Lord than the one who loves you so much He died to save you.

Followers of a lord like Darth Vader can only be bad. With Jesus as your Lord, you are made good. When the Lord Jesus frees His people from their sins and from death, He also frees them to have clean hearts and live a new life. No other lord can do that! That's how you know Jesus is the real Lord.

Journal:

How does a bad lord treat the people under his care? How does a good lord treat people?

Pray:

Lord Jesus, You are the master of everything. Please protect me from bad lords who would hurt me. Help me to trust and follow You always. Amen.   R. C.

Knit Together

Have you ever watched someone knit a scarf or a sweater? The knitter follows a pattern. The pattern might say when to change yarn colors, so the scarf will have stripes. The pattern could tell the knitter to change the kind of stitch he or she is making, so the sweater will have fuzzy bumps. Knitters don't make random stitches and hope the yarn will turn into something useful. They know what they want to make, and they have a plan for how to do it.

The Bible tells us that God makes people by knitting them together. He doesn't knit us with needles and yarn. He builds the elements He created into proteins, cells, tissues, organs, and systems to make every person. He designs the genes that give a person stripes or fuzzy bumps . . . or a big smile or black hair. God's pattern is Himself. He makes every person in His own image.

When Adam and Eve sinned, they lost the goodness of God's image. But God loves us too much to let sin ruin us. Jesus lived a perfect life for us. He died on the cross to give us His righteousness. When He comes back for us, His holiness will be knit into us forever like stripes in a scarf. God's works are wonderful!

For You formed my inward parts; You knitted me together in my mother's womb. I praise You, for I am fearfully and wonderfully made. Wonderful are Your works; my soul knows it very well. My frame was not hidden from You, when I was being made in secret, intricately woven in the depths of the earth.

Psalm 139:13–15

Journal:

Do you know someone who knits, builds, or makes things? What is something you would like to learn to make?

Pray:

Lord God, heavenly Father, thank You for knitting me together to give me life. Keep me in the true faith always, and remake me with Jesus' everlasting righteousness. Amen.

R. C.

We All Love Love

Love is patient and kind; love does not envy or boast; it is not arrogant or rude. It does not insist on its own way; it is not irritable or resentful; it does not rejoice at wrongdoing, but rejoices with the truth.

1 Corinthians 13:4–6

First Corinthians 13 is known as "the love chapter," because it's all about love. It's often chosen for a reading at weddings. Maybe you've seen parts of it on a bulletin board at church or painted on a sign at home. We all love love!

But what if we got more specific? What if the love chapter gave some examples, like this:

Love is nice to the kid who always needs the directions repeated.

Love is happy for the person who wins the science fair, even when it isn't you.

Love doesn't brag when you win the free throw contest.

Love doesn't think you know better than your teacher or your parents.

Love doesn't make bathroom jokes during Sunday School.

Love doesn't get growly when someone skips your turn.

Love doesn't laugh when people are saying mean things about someone.

Suddenly love doesn't seem so nice! Although we like love, none of us are born good at it. The only way we know how to love is if God teaches us. The most loving thing that has ever happened is when Jesus gave His life for us on the cross to forgive our sins. We meant so much to Him that He gave up everything to be near us. For sinners, love always means forgiving one another. God shows us how to do that by doing it Himself.

Journal:

Name someone you know who is especially loving. What are the ways that he or she shows love?

Pray:

Dear Lord Jesus, thank You for showing us what love is. Help me to love other people enough to forgive them like You forgave me. Amen.   R. C.

Jesus the Comforter

Sad things happen to everyone. We lose things and break things. We get a bad grade, or we don't make the team. We have to move away from our friends. Worst of all, people die.

We wish sad things would just go away. Usually, that doesn't happen. Sin is a part of us as long as we live, and all our sadness is because of our sin.

But you know who pays for our sin: Jesus. He died on the cross to forgive us and rose to life so that we will rise from the dead. Jesus also comforts us in our "affliction," or sad things. He lived on this sad earth and knows about every sad thing that happens. He got bad marks from the Pharisees, and they didn't want Him on their team. He had no place to live. His friend Judas became his enemy. He cried when His friend Lazarus died.

This means that Jesus hurts when you hurt. He knows what your sadness feels like, because He has felt it Himself. He cares because He loves you. Maybe someday, someone you love will have a sadness you've felt. You can share that person's sadness like Jesus shares yours.

Blessed be the God and Father of our Lord Jesus Christ, the Father of mercies and God of all comfort, who comforts us in all our affliction, so that we may be able to comfort those who are in any affliction, with the comfort with which we ourselves are comforted by God.

2 Corinthians 1:3-4

Journal:

What's a sad thing that has happened to you? Who helped you through it?

Pray:

Dear Jesus, thank You for living in this sad world so that someday we would never feel sad again. Help me to be a good friend to other people when they are sad. Amen.   *R. C.*

But thanks be to God, who in Christ always leads us in triumphal procession, and through us spreads the fragrance of the knowledge of Him everywhere. For we are the aroma of Christ to God among those who are being saved and among those who are perishing.

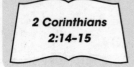

2 Corinthians 2:14–15

What's That Smell?

When you walk into someone's house, what's one of the first things you notice? I bet it's the smell. You can tell if someone has been baking cookies, if the dog got in a fight with a skunk, or what kind of oil is in the diffuser. There's a lot to learn just inside someone's door, even before you start looking around and listening.

You have a smell too. The way you act can be like your gym shoes or shampoo. The things you talk about and the way you talk about them give a whiff of you. So do your favorite books and movies. Are your words careful and kind? That's a breath of fresh air! Do you watch shows full of rotten people acting rotten? That stinks!

It's a lot of responsibility to be the "aroma of Christ." Nobody wants to smell bad! Good news: in Baptism, you were washed and made new. When you confess your sins and trust that you have Jesus' forgiveness, you are renewed. Jesus allows you to live in righteousness and purity forever. You can breathe a big sigh of relief for that.

Journal:

What's your favorite thing to smell when you walk in your door at home?

Pray:

Dear Lord Jesus, there is nothing good in me without You. Please forgive me for my sins against You and my neighbors. Renew me to live in the way You would have me live. Amen. R. C.

Answer When Called

Whom do you turn to when you need help? Does that person always answer you when you call? Sometimes we can feel alone in our struggles, as if people aren't listening to us or don't care.

Sometimes we're the ones who aren't listening. Have you ever ignored a friend in need? When we don't listen to another's call, that person might feel alone or without help.

Our psalm today talks about someone else who had troubles. David had many enemies, but he knew where to turn. He prayed to God, knowing that God always listens to our prayers. Even when other people aren't listening to us and we feel alone, we can pray to our good and gracious God, who always hears us for Jesus' sake.

No matter what situation you're in, God is in control and listening to your call. And next time someone else needs a listening ear, remember to pray with them and show them you care! You can pray together to the God who cares for you both.

Answer me when I call, O God of my righteousness! You have given me relief when I was in distress. Be gracious to me and hear my prayer!

Psalm 4:1

Journal:

What can you do to listen better to others?

Pray:

Dear God, help me to listen when others speak to me. Thank You for always hearing me when I call to You. Amen.   *M. G.*

Finally, be strong in the Lord and in the strength of His might.

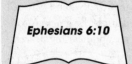

Ephesians 6:10

Are You Strong Enough?

Many people judge others based on strength and weakness. How does it make you feel when someone looks at you and says, "There is no way you are strong enough to do that!"

Satan wants us to feel that we cannot succeed because of our weakness. This is where Satan falls on his face.

In Paul's Letter to the Ephesians, God tells us to put our faith in His strength. God is strong enough to cleanse us of our sins. God is strong enough to carry us through troubling times in our life. He has done all this through the death and resurrection of His only Son, Jesus.

While we may not be able to lift a box or move a table with Godlike might, God strengthens us by His unfailing love. His love for us is so great that He sent His own Son, Jesus, to be our Savior from sin. This love will help us each and every day.

Journal:

How does being weaker than others make you feel? How does being stronger than others make you feel?

Pray:

Dear Lord, help me to be strong in my faith every day. In Your name I pray. Amen.   *M. G.*

Turn Away

A habit of sin is extremely hard to break. Sin comes in many different shapes, such as misusing food and technology or gossiping. Sin tells us it surely will not matter if you take another cookie for dessert, play on your device a little longer than you were allowed, or talk about someone in an unkind way.

Unfortunately, these sins and many others are a part of our daily lives. We find it impossible to turn away from them and follow the righteous path.

God sent His Son to clean up our sinful nature. Jesus died on the cross to wash away our sin. By faith, we receive forgiveness through Jesus' sacrifice. Faith does not keep us from sinning, but it does promise us the way to eternal salvation. God empowers us through His Word to turn away from our sins and follow the example set before us in the Ten Commandments. We can trust in God each and every day.

When God saw what they did, how they turned from their evil way, God relented of the disaster that He had said He would do to them, and He did not do it.

Jonah 3:10

Journal:

What is one way God helps us turn away from sin?

Pray:

God, help me to turn away from my sins through the power of the Spirit. Amen.

M. G.

AUGUST

28

Wednesday

I will restore the fortunes of My people Israel, and they shall rebuild the ruined cities and inhabit them; they shall plant vineyards and drink their wine, and they shall make gardens and eat their fruit.

Amos 9:14

Fresh Food

There is nothing like having fresh food for a meal. For some, planting and tending to a garden is a way to provide this for them. From planting the seeds all the way to harvest, these plants are well cared for by their owners. It is an amazing thing to partake in the fruits of one's labor.

In today's lesson, we learn about how God restores and provides for His people. This is done not because His people deserve this treatment but out of fatherly goodness. God provides for His people each and every day in a variety of ways. From the money we make to the gardens we grow, God gives us all that we need and own. All of this came at a price, but it was a price God was willing to pay. God gave His only Son to die on the cross so that we may live with Him in heaven.

When we enjoy fresh food, remember that while it may have been tended by your hands, it is a blessing from our heavenly Father!

Journal:

How do you thank God for the things in your life?

Pray:

God, I thank You for the gifts You have given me. In Jesus' name. Amen.

M. G.

The Versus Battle

Have you ever had a this-versus-that battle? Maybe it was this sports team versus that team, or this book series versus that series. Sometimes a this-versus-that battle can spark the silliest arguments!

We have opinions on a lot of things. However, we should not allow these opinions to harm our ability to share the love of Jesus with others. As Christians, we can treat others with respect, in the kindest way possible, showing them the love of Jesus. Don't let petty disagreements define your personal character. Let the teachings of Scripture guide you in all things.

When someone wants to get into a this-versus-that battle, understand that there may be no right or wrong answer. If the disagreement is about matters of the faith, know that the most important truth is that Jesus died for everyone. His death and resurrection is yours through His gift of faith. By faith, you will enjoy eternal life with Him.

As for the one who is weak in faith, welcome him, but not to quarrel over opinions.

Romans 14:1

Journal:

What is the best way to handle someone who wants to have a this-versus-that battle with you?

Pray:

Dear Father in heaven, help me reflect Your love the next time I disagree with someone. Amen. M. G.

To the Lord our God belong mercy and forgiveness, for we have rebelled against Him and have not obeyed the voice of the LORD our God by walking in His laws, which He set before us by His servants the prophets.

Daniel 9:9–10

Why Do We Rebel?

What thing do you hate the most? When I was growing up, it was condiments. I wanted everything to be plain without any additives. Whenever something had ketchup, mustard, or anything other than what I wanted, I was not fun to be around. How do you react when something you don't like shows up in front of you?

In our sin, we adamantly reject the goodness of God's creation. It is in our sinful nature to rebel against things in this world, such as rules, authority, and even God's Word. Even though we create divisions among our brothers and sisters in Christ, there is still salvation in Christ's death and resurrection. Our rebellious nature meets its match, and we are absolved of our sins through God's only Son, Jesus.

The next time you find yourself in one of those moods, look to Christ and be comforted that there is always forgiveness.

Journal:

What is something you can do to positively affect those around you when you feel rebellious?

Pray:

Dear heavenly Father, please ease my fears that cause me to rebel against You and this world. Amen.
                                                                    M. G.

That Silly Stain

One of the things I hated most when I was a child was going to school with a stain on my clothes. Most of the time, it was grass stains from recess the previous week. It made me feel as if my clothes were not good enough for my friends. I worried that others would pick on me for having dirty clothes. This is how the stain of sin should feel to everyone in this world. Sin is the dirty, nasty thing that follows us around and gives others an opportunity to point out our faults. On our own, we cannot do anything to erase this stain that has been with us our whole lives.

Therefore, beloved, since you are waiting for these, be diligent to be found by Him without spot or blemish, and at peace.

2 Peter 3:14

With this kind of thinking, one could believe that people would remain depressed throughout their entire life. God's Word in 2 Peter tells us that there is hope for us! Through Christ, we are cleansed of our sin and no longer need to endure its weight upon our shoulders. God's sacrifice of His only Son gives a new birth and hope of eternal life in heaven.

So wear that stain well because through Christ we are no longer lost and condemned people. We are God's chosen people—washed clean of all sin's stain at our Baptism.

Journal:

How do you let stains affect you? What will you say to the friend or family member who has a stain on his or her clothes?

Pray:

Dear Father, thank You for washing me clean of my sin. Amen.   M. G.

August

Bible puzzles, games, and activities

Solutions on page 120

Discover Zone: Growing Seeds

Materials: 2 cups, seeds, soil, spoon, water

Directions: Put your name on two cups. Mark cups with a 1 or a 2. Plant seeds in each cup.

My Plan: Circle the growing condition you will test:

Water   Light   Soil

Other: _____

To test this condition, Plant 1 will

_____

Plant 2 will

_____

My Guess: This is what I think will happen:

_____

_____

Observations (what I see each day)

Day	Plant 1	Plant 2
1		
2		
3		
4		
5		

Findings. Tell what happened and why.

_____

_____

_____

_____

_____

_____

_____

_____

_____

_____

What Did the Lamb of God Do for You?

Directions: Use the code to find a Bible verse that answers the question.

B_____ , _____ _____
12, 7, 19, 6, 2, 18   3, 19, 7   2, 5, 17, 12

_____ _____ , _____ _____
6, 16   1, 6, 18   11, 19, 6   3, 5, 13, 7, 10

_____ _____ _____
5, 11, 5, 4   3, 19, 7   10, 14, 8

_____ _____ _____ .
6, 16   3, 19, 7   11, 6, 15, 2, 18

_____ 1:29
9, 6, 19, 8

Code:

A = 5
B = 12
D = 18
E = 7
F = 16
G = 1
H = 19
I = 14
J = 9
K = 13
L = 2
M = 17
N = 8
O = 6
R = 15
S = 10
T = 3
W = 11
Y = 4

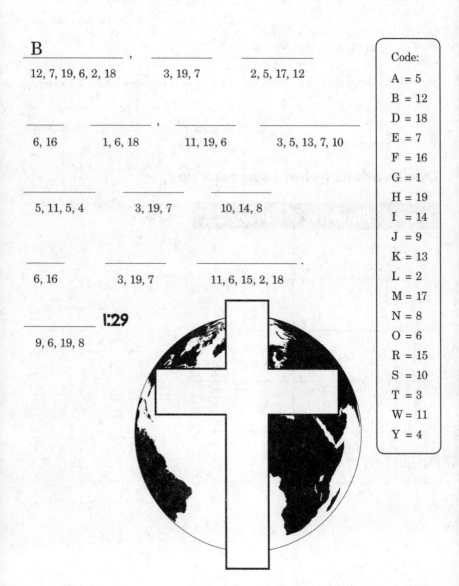

117

My Coloring Page

August Journal

Puzzle 1 Answer

Discover Zone: Growing Seeds

Materials: 2 cups, seeds, soil, spoon, water

Directions: Put your name on two cups. Mark cups with a 1 or a 2. Plant seeds in each cup.

My Plan: Circle the growing condition you will test:

Water   Light   Soil

Other: _____

To test this condition, Plant 1 will
Answers will vary.

Plant 2 will

My Guess: This is what I think will happen:

Observations (what I see each day)

Day	Plant 1	Plant 2
1	Answers will vary.	
2		
3		
4		
5		

Findings. Tell what happened and why.
Answers will vary.

Puzzle 2 Answer

What Did the Lamb of God Do for You?

Directions: Use the code to find a Bible verse that answers the question.

BEHOLD   THE   LAMB
12, 7, 19, 6, 2, 18   3, 19, 7   2, 5, 17, 12

OF   GOD   WHO   TAKES
6, 16   1, 6, 18   11, 19, 6   3, 5, 13, 7, 10

AWAY   THE   SIN
5, 11, 5, 4   3, 19, 7   10, 14, 8

OF   THE   WORLD
6, 16   3, 19, 7   11, 6, 15, 2, 18

JOHN   1:29
9, 6, 19, 8

Code:
A = 5
B = 12
D = 38
E = 7
F = 16
G = 1
H = 19
I = 14
J = 9
K = 13
L = 2
M = 17
N = 8
O = 6
R = 15
S = 10
T = 3
W = 11
Y = 4

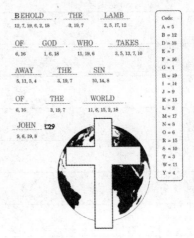